MIRACLE MATH

MIRACLE MATH

By

Harry Lorayne

BARNES
&NOBLE
BOOKS
NEW YORK

1992 Barnes & Noble Books

ISBN 0-88029-876-6

Printed and bound in the United States of America

M 10 9 8 7 6 5 4

CONTENTS

Foreword

Miracle Mathematics is a cinch, once you know the secrets and techniques. I'll show you how to master mathematics and save priceless minutes and hours . . . build your qualifications for that raise or that new job . . . save dollars at the store . . . double your power to solve problems automatically — for all time.

"The very hairs of your head are all numbered."

— Matthew, X:30

Would you like to be able to add long columns of grocery receipts or business expenses in a flash . . . and prove even faster that your answer is correct? If you earn a commission, can you estimate — mentally — the dollar share of every sale you make?

And what would you give to be able to solve any financial or business problem easier, faster, and surer than anyone else in your office?

If you're willing to listen to what I've got to tell you in these pages, I'll prove to you that mathematics is a cinch, once you know the secrets of the meaning of numbers! I'll show you how to master the techniques of calculation that have made millions of dollars for others, by enabling them to compete for better jobs, to make important decisions at the drop of a mathematical hat, to be confident because they knew, beyond a shadow of a digital doubt, that their figures were right.

What will a firm command of mathematics do for you? It will guide you, product by product and saving by saving, through the supermarket. It will let you estimate, rapidly and accurately, how many more games the Yankees must win to clinch the pennant. It will prove to your boss that your plan for expanding a program is the most practical, economical, and promising. It will let you save precious minutes when you've got to solve problems such as these:

Add $25.46, $44.05, $18.75. $93.27, and $403.02.

How much will it cost to buy 350 ball bearings, if they cost 3-1/2¢ each?

If two basketball teams played at a rate of one basket every 20 seconds, how many points would be scored in a 48-minute game?

If you have to travel 150 miles in 2-1/2 hours, how fast must you drive?

How much will the wool for a sweater cost, if the pattern requires fourteen balls, and the wool you like is 69¢ a ball?

Skill in mathematics can do all this for you and much more, if you'll just let me show you how to make it work for you. With the mathematical miracles described in this book you'll add long columns of figures as quickly as you can read! You'll multiply without carrying a single number! You'll subtract with little more effort than writing down the problems! You'll do long-division problems in the bat of an eye — perfectly!

And you'll do your adding, subtracting, and multiplying in a much <u>surer</u> and easier way than you've ever done before — <u>from left to right!</u>

Adding as quickly as you read . . . multiplying without carrying . . . working from left to right. . . . Does this sound different to you? You bet it does! But <u>vive la différence</u> that can bring you to the attention of your associates at work, open up new career possibilities for you, cut your paperwork time by two-thirds, save you money when you shop, even make you the center of attraction as you amaze your friends with your mathematical dexterity.

Don't get me wrong — you don't have to throw out the mathematics you've been taught up to now, or spend time learning a strange new system of figures. Nothing like that at all. Your grade-school teacher taught you the basic elements of our numerical system, and the hours and hours of practice you put into addition, subtraction, multiplication, and division tables will still stand you in good stead.

But why drive around in an old Model T just because that was the car you learned on? Why work out your arithmetic problems the long way, when great computer-age advances have been made in calculation, and you can use these modern mathematical tools to cut your time — and work — in half?

The mathematical miracles that I'll show you in the following chapters are simply the natural developments of the modernization — the evolution — of mathematics, just as the Model T gave way to the streamlined sports cars of today. What I'll show you is how to streamline your mathematics, and get to your answers faster and safer!

Now I know it is not particularly easy to change habits that have been with you most of your life. If you have never been introduced to these modern miracle methods, they may seem a bit strange to you at first.

At first — and only at first — the old Model T methods may seem easier to you. But only because they are more familiar to you at the moment.

Don't be fooled. Learn and use these new methods for just a short time — and you will see how much faster, easier, and more accurate they definitely are. How useful they are to you immediately. And how, before you know it, they actually become second nature to you.

The lessons in <u>Miracle Mathematics</u> have been carefully and scientifically planned to yield breath-taking results through self-instruction and self-teaching. The book is easy to use, and I'll explain each step and each section completely. As you learn, you'll be able to see how much you've learned and how well you're doing with the aid of self-review quizzes and problems. And you'll be cautioned against going on until you've thoroughly grasped the subject at hand.

Before you've finished, you'll have mastered every secret, every technique, every mathematical miracle I've described. The mathematical short cuts that can change your life will have become second nature to you. So let's not delay your introduction to <u>Mathematical Miracle Number One</u> another instant . . . .

<u>SPECIAL NOTE</u>: As you will soon see for yourself, this book is different from most books in a very special way. <u>It wants you to talk back to it.</u> It <u>demands</u> that you actively participate in what's going on. It asks you to pick up a pencil and work out your answers right on its pages.

In other words, this book makes you <u>think.</u> Not just passively read, but actively <u>learn</u> what's on its pages. It makes you <u>think</u> about what you've learned. And it burns these short cuts into your mind in the exercises, drills, and questions that it asks you on almost every other page.

In this way, you make sure that you understand every point. You have a chance to correct errors immediately, and to put what you've learned to work for you on the very same page. This simple idea — of writing on the pages of this book, of turning this book into a conversation where you can show yourself how much you've learned — can double the benefits you get out of its pages.

Start proving that to yourself right now.

CHAPTER ONE

Mathematical Miracle Number One—How To Add Faster Than An Adding Machine

"The lowest limit in enumeration among primitive peoples is among the Yancos, an Amazon tribe who cannot count beyond poettarrarorincoaroac, which is their word for 'three.'"

— "The Guinness Book of World Records"

I'll begin by making two assumptions:

First, that unlike the Yancos you can count beyond three — all the way up to . . . 18.

Second, that you're willing to spend sixty seconds to learn a simple trick with a pencil, and then practice that trick for a few short minutes until you can perform it as easily as you speak your name.

And I can promise you this — that that simple trick with a pencil will eliminate the single biggest stumbling block in addition: carrying too many figures in your head.

HOW MANY NUMBERS CAN YOUR
MIND HOLD AT ONCE?

Before I tell you the secret, however, let me show
you the reason that it had to be developed. I'd like you
to try a simple experiment with me right now. First,
let's try dealing with numbers — the hard way.

Take a look at the following two-digit numbers. Read
them only once.

27, 81, 34, 19, 62

Now look away from the book and try to repeat them
from memory.

Could you do it?

Few people can. Those two-digit numbers are just
too big to be held in your mind. And yet this impossible stunt is just what you try to do every time you add
a column of figures the ordinary way!

Those who have read my book "How to Develop a
Super-Power Memory" will realize that memorizing
two-digit numbers is not impossible or especially difficult. However, I'm not teaching the art of memory
here, and I don't think memory systems are necessary
in simple mathematics.

For example, if I asked you to add the following
column of figures, wouldn't you do it this way:

8 Eight,

7 plus seven are fifteen,

3 plus three are eighteen,

6 plus six are twenty-four . . . .

See? You're trying to carry two-digit numbers in your head every time you add even a simple column of figures — if you do it the old way.

But now, look at the following single-digit numbers. Again, read them just once. Then look away and try to repeat them from memory.

Here they are:

7, 1, 4, 9, 2

Now look away and repeat them from memory.

Could you do it this time? Of course! Now you have seen for yourself how much easier — and how much faster — it is to remember single digits than those cumbersome double digits in the first experiments. But do you understand why it's so much easier?

Because the human mind is equipped to carry just so much information at one time.

If you overload your mind, the result will be a "short-circuit" — forgetfulness or confusion. When you feed too many figures into your mind at one time . . . when you try to carry two-digit numbers in your head as you add a column of figures, it's only natural and human to forget them, confuse them, make mistakes, and have to start all over.

So, the problem becomes: How to eliminate those two-digit numbers forever. And the solution becomes: That trick with a pencil that I mentioned at the beginning of this chapter. The secret is simply this:

Dot equals Ten.

"." = 10

·   = 10

The dot is the key to freeing your mind from the unnecessary task of storing numbers upon numbers, of trying to juggle two-digit numbers which your mind simply cannot retain.

Just as this symbol, ////, helps the proverbial jailbird to keep track of the days by counting in fives instead of single days, the dot will help you keep track of the tens you've added, so that you can turn all of your mental power to adding single digits — never more than a pair at a time — almost as quickly as your eye, flying down a column of figures, can take them in!

And all because · = 10.

THE JAPANESE "WIZARDS"

In Japan they've known this secret of rapid calculation for hundreds of years. A Japanese bookkeeper, when he's figuring out the answers to his arithmetical problems, doesn't try to wrestle with cumbersome two-digit numbers in his mind. He uses a specially designed device to do the remembering for him — a simple instrument of beads and rods called an abacus.

Every bead in each row on the abacus has a certain value. When the Japanese bookkeeper wants to add a column of figures, all he does is move the correct combination of beads, and the totals and subtotals automatically take care of themselves.

In this way the abacus acts as the bookkeeper's memory — doing all the remembering for him while he concentrates only on combining numbers — remember, never more than a pair at a time — more quickly than you'd believe possible.

Stories of how abacus operators in Japan have been able to outspeed the U. S. Army's most modern electric calculators are plentiful. The reason for this seemingly

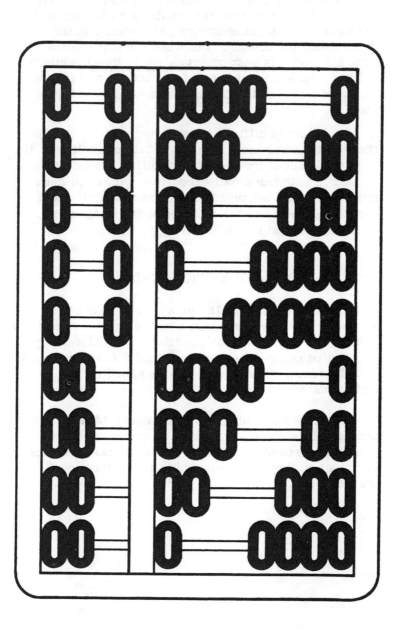

impossible fact is really quite simple. It took the abacus operator and the calculator operator exactly the same time to record the numbers contained in the problem — the Japanese moved his beads and the soldier pushed his buttons. But when the Japanese had done his part, his answer was already there; while the soldier still had to push the Total button, and then wait a fifth of a second for the machine to spit out the answer.

The Japanese attitude toward numbers — the idea that by recording the number you automatically add it — is the basis of the secret of addition I'm talking about . . . with one small exception: you won't even need an abacus, because the dot you make with your pencil will be one of the most effective weapons you've ever leveled against misbehaving numbers.

HOW THE DOT CARRIES THE LOAD

After I've taught you the proper way to use the secret — · = 10 — you won't juggle numbers mentally ever again. And, with the practice in combining digits that you're going to be getting in just a few pages, you'll soon be adding huge columns more speedily than an adding machine.

Let's look again at the old-fashioned, Model T way of adding. Here's another column of numbers, accompanied by a rough translation of the mental gyrations you must go through if you add in the conventional manner:

3 Three

4 and four are seven,

5 and five are twelve,

7 and seven are nineteen,

6 and six are twenty-five,

2 and two are twenty-seven,

9 and nine are thirty-six

1 and one makes thirty-seven

<u>5</u> and five makes

42 forty-two!

Wouldn't it be much simpler if all you had to think, because of a dot and a few moments of practice, was <u>Seven . . . dot-two . . . nine . . . dot-five . . . seven . . . dot-six . . . seven . . . dot-two . . . forty-two!</u>

Let's see what all this dot mumbo-jumbo actually means. Let's add this same column of figures in our new, simple way.

The first two digits in the column (3 and 4) <u>become</u> 7.

Now you combine this 7 with another 5; and you're holding a 12 on your mind.

But what about that magic key to miraculous adding: " · " = 10? If that's really so, then 12 must equal ·2, & ·2 must equal 12. Instead of carrying the 12 with you to the next digit, <u>this time</u> see it as ·2. Put the dot down, right next to the 5 (to remind yourself that you've reached more than 10), and then continue to add the remaining single digit 2 to the next number in the column.

Do you understand? The basic principle is as simple as this:

1. Make a dot beside (to the left of) every
    number in the column that takes you to
    ten or above in the course of adding; and

2. Then add only the remaining digit to the
    next number in the column.

Every time you combine two digits that equal ten or
more, you simply record the ten with a <u>dot</u> — forget
that ten and keep on adding. And now you'll be adding
the <u>remaining single digit</u> to the next number in the
column.

This short cut is perfectly legal, because · = 10.
Whenever you add 7 and 8 from now on, your answer
will be ·5. The total of 9 and 4 will no longer be 13 to
you, it will be ·3. And 6 and 4 now equal ·0 (or, if you
prefer, just plain dot). 8 and 6 = ·4; 7 and 9 = ·6; 5
and 6 = ·1; 7 and 4 = ·1; and so on.

So now our sample problem looks like this:

	3	
	4	Seven,
	· 5	dot-two,
	7	nine,
	· 6	dot-five
	2	seven,
(Now glance up the	· 9	dot-six,
column in	1	seven
one instant to count	· 5	dot-two
(four <u>dots</u>)	42	forty-two!

Now you can see how <u>the dot does the carrying for</u>

you, leaving your mind free to do nothing more than
such simple additions as 3 plus 4 = 7, 7 plus 5 = ·2, 2
plus 7 = 9, 9 plus 6 = ·5, 5 plus 2 = 7, and so on down
the entire column. Then, when you've reached the bottom and all you have on your mind is a 2, write that 2
under the line, and simply write a 4 (for the four dots
that you made) to arrive at 42! Remember, · = 10.
Four dots (· · · ·) equals 40.

So, to make this perfectly clear to you, let's review
the last step: After adding the last two single digits
(7 + 5 = ·2), make the dot to the left of the 5, and then
record the answer (2) below the line. Now, simply run
your eye up the column, counting the dots. In this example, there are four dots. Write a 4 in front of the 2,
and you have the complete answer — 42.

TRY IT OUT FOR YOURSELF

If this sounds strange to you at first, that's just because you haven't tried it yet. Why don't you take a
few seconds now to prove to yourself that you're a better mathematician right this minute than you were five
pages ago! Pick up a pencil, and run through the
following columns of digits, just to get the hang of adding with this new technique.

Remember — mark a dot just to the left of every
number that brings you to ten or over, and then simply
continue your addition with the remaining digit. For
example, see a 5 and a 9 as dot 4; mark the dot beside
the 9, and add only the 4 to the next number in the column.

Ready? Take your time — right now I'm only interested in your understanding the technique — as you
practice what I've taught you, with:

DRILL IN ADDING WITHOUT CARRYING
(OR HOW TO USE THE DOT)

	1.	4		2.	2
		• 7			8
		• 9			4
		1	Now		6
		4	you do it		5
Like this		• 8			9
		3			6
		1			9
		• 6			5
		• 9			8
		52			

	3.	6		4.	5
		5			5
		7			6
		7			5
		5			6
		9			1
		7			6
		9			8
		5			4
		1			2

5.	7	6.	8
	7		5
	7		6
	8		1
	1		9
	3		4
	4		8
	8		6
	3		5
	6		2

7.	6	8.	5
	6		9
	6		6
	2		5
	9		8
	2		1
	6		4
	5		7
	6		7
	3		4

9.		10.	
	3		1
	2		8
	6		6
	7		3
	7		6
	3		5
	3		9
	6		7
	8		9
	5		6

11.		12.	
	4		7
	8		8
	3		3
	8		8
	8		7
	7		7
	6		4
	9		9
	9		1
	9		9

13.	1	14.	9
	9		5
	3		5
	1		6
	1		2
	5		5
	3		1
	9		9
	8		7
	9		9

15.	9	16.	9
	1		9
	4		9
	9		9
	4		9
	7		9
	9		6
	9		9
	9		9
	9		9

17.	8	18.	7
	8		7
	8		7
	8		7
	8		7
	8		7
	2		8
	8		7
	8		7
	8		7

19.	6	20.	5
	6		5
	6		5
	6		5
	6		5
	6		5
	4		5
	6		5
	6		5
	6		5

(Note: The answers to all drill problems in this
book can be found on page 232).

Simple? Of course! That's what miracle mathematics is all about — simplicity in working with numbers. Attacking each arithmetic problem armed with the streamlining "miracle" that will give you the answer most quickly, easily and accurately.

(Please, even though you do understand the dot idea perfectly, do not proceed until you've completed the above drill. Complete all the drills in this book. If you don't, you're defeating the entire purpose; mine and yours!)

HOW THIS SIMPLE TRICK MAKES ALL
ADDITION A SNAP!

Just by knowing the simple secret of recording 10's with dots as you add a column of digits, you're already well on the way toward tremendously increasing your adding speed.

But the really big payoff of that little trick is in the new use to which you'll be able to put your free-from-carrying mind! With a row of dots keeping tabs on the number of tens you've already added up, you'll always be able to concentrate on nothing more than the simplest kind of addition — 3 + 4, 9 + 3, 8 + 5 — one pair at a time. Your over-all task of adding a column of numbers is thus automatically reduced to an easy series of simple one-digit additions.

And there are only 45 such simple one-digit additions in all the problems you will ever have to solve!

If you can add up to 18, you can solve any addition problem that could ever be put to you, because with the dot technique you'll never have to add more than two single-digit numbers at a time, and the highest that two such numbers can total is 18.

After all, there are only nine digits — 1, 2, 3, 4, 5, 6, 7, 8 and 9. And that means only 45 possible combinations of two numbers, from 1 + 1 to 9 + 9. If you know the answers to all these combinations — at a glance — adding will never be any harder for you than reading!

And there's one more big advantage that makes this new system even easier. In 20 of these 45 combinations — the ones which add up to 9 or less — <u>the answers that you learned in school are all you'll ever need to know.</u>   3 + 4 = 7, and you add them just as you always have. But when you run across two numbers that add up to more than 10 — like 8 + 6 — you simply switch to this dot system. 8 + 6 = ·4; 6 + 5 = ·1; 7 + 8 = ·5; 9 + 3 = ·2; and so on.

On the next page is a table of these 45 single-digit combinations and the answers. Learn them right now — so well that the answer pops into your mind automatically, on sight, whenever you tackle an addition problem:

1 + 1 = 2

1 + 2 = 3
2 + 2 = 4

1 + 3 = 4
2 + 3 = 5
3 + 3 = 6

1 + 4 = 5
2 + 4 = 6
3 + 4 = 7
4 + 4 = 8

1 + 5 = 6
2 + 5 = 7
3 + 5 = 8
4 + 5 = 9
5 + 5 = .

1 + 6 = 7
2 + 6 = 8
3 + 6 = 9
4 + 6 = .
5 + 6 = ·1
6 + 6 = ·2

1 + 7 = 8
2 + 7 = 9
3 + 7 = .
4 + 7 = ·1
5 + 7 = ·2
6 + 7 = ·3
7 + 7 = ·4

1 + 8 = 9
2 + 8 = .
3 + 8 = ·1
4 + 8 = ·2
5 + 8 = ·3
6 + 8 = ·4
7 + 8 = ·5
8 + 8 = ·6

1 + 9 = .
2 + 9 = ·1
3 + 9 = ·2
4 + 9 = ·3
5 + 9 = ·4
6 + 9 = ·5
7 + 9 = ·6
8 + 9 = ·7
9 + 9 = ·8

Do you understand what I've done here? The answers to those combinations which equal 10 or more are translated into their immediately usable (for addition) dot-forms. Now you can look at a column of figures and deduce its sum without ever thinking of a number higher than 9!

With the help of a couple of dots, you can actually read addition — run your eyes quickly down the page, always keeping a running tally as you speed to the end of the column faster than you ever believed possible.

All you've got to do now is put in a bit of practice combining these digits — until you see the most useful of the answers — dot-forms — automatically. Drill yourself until you can look at a 6 and a 7 and know ·3. You did the greatest part of this drilling in grade school; now, all you're working for is speed.

Let's have a little practice. Here are these 45 combinations again. You fill in the answers, using the dots each time you meet two numbers that add to 10 or more.

DRILL IN RAPID DIGIT COMBINATION

1.   4 + 7 = ·1   2.   1 + 8 =

3.   3 + 3 =   4.   6 + 6 =

5.   4 + 3 =   6.   7 + 9 =

7.   6 + 3 =   8.   8 + 2 =

9.   8 + 8 =   10.   3 + 8 =

11.   8 + 4 =   12.   6 + 6 =

13.   9 + 2 =   14.   9 + 9 =

15.   8 + 3 =   16.   8 + 3 =

17.   9 + 3 =   18.   7 + 4 =

19. $7 + 7 =$ 20. $9 + 7 =$

21. $6 + 1 =$ 22. $6 + 6 =$

23. $6 + 4 =$ 24. $6 + 6 =$

25. $5 + 7 =$ 26. $9 + 9 =$

27. $7 + 8 =$ 28. $5 + 8 =$

29. $5 + 5 =$ 30. $8 + 4 =$

31. $6 + 5 =$ 32. $8 + 7 =$

33. $9 + 9 =$ 34. $4 + 8 =$

35. 4 + 7 =   36. 4 + 7 =

37. 2 + 9 =   38. 1 + 1 =

39. 3 + 9 =   40. 9 + 8 =

41. 9 + 6 =   42. 3 + 8 =

43. 3 + 7 =   44. 2 + 9 =

45. 8 + 8 =   46. 4 + 8 =

47. 9 + 7 =   48. 4 + 9 =

49. 5 + 9 =   50. 2 + 6 =

How did you do? Well enough to race the clock with a few problems in adding long columns? Try these on for size:

DRILL IN RAPID COLUMN ADDITION

1.   3
        6
       •6
        2
       •9
       •6
        7
       •1
        6
       •4
      5 0

2.   6
        4
        5
        7
        7
        3
        8
        4
        2
        6

3.	4	4.	9
	8		1
	8		7
	9		5
	1		6
	3		3
	1		9
	8		8
	3		7
	6		4

5.	8	6.	1
	9		9
	1		9
	7		4
	4		8
	7		5
	8		8
	8		6
	5		3
	4		6

7.	8		8.	7
	9			5
	4			3
	8			6
	6			9
	7			5
	6			4
	5			3
	4			7
	6			4

9.	5		10.	2
	6			2
	7			2
	4			9
	9			8
	7			5
	3			9
	7			5
	4			6
	4			6

WHAT HAVE YOU LEARNED SO FAR?

Before I begin explaining the next phase of addition, I want you to be absolutely certain that you understand everything you've read up to this page. Let's go back briefly and review what you've learned.

To begin with, the trouble with old-fashioned addition is that it makes you try to remember two-digit numbers all the time. This is unnecessary, and our new system lets you get the same results — remembering nothing more than single digits. This means that you're able to work faster, more accurately, and with greater confidence.

What's the secret? Mathematical Miracle Number 1: Make a dot beside every number that takes you to 10 or above in the course of adding, and then go on to add only the remaining digit.

The dot does the remembering for you, and you gain new speed through concentration on adding just one-digit numbers, never more than two at a time. And, since there are only 45 possible combinations of one-digit numbers, you need only master those combinations to be able to add faster than an adding machine!

REVIEW QUIZ NO. 1

If you can't answer all of the following questions, go back to the beginning of this chapter and review the sections that you haven't fully understood. Remember: the only good mark is 100%.

[1.] How high must I be able to add if I use the dot method of adding?

[2.] How much is a dot worth?

[3.] How many digits is the most I'll ever
have to work with in a single operation,
with the <u>dot</u> method?

[4.] Exactly what is the purpose of the <u>dot</u>?

[5.] When using <u>dots</u>, will I ever have to remember more than one remaining number
at a time?

[6.] Do I thoroughly understand what I've
read and learned so far?

ANSWERS:

[1.] To 18 — no higher.

[2.] 10.

[3.] Only two digits at a time — never more.

[4.] To mark down on the paper the fact that
you've added over 10. The dot remem-
bers that 10 for you — carries that 10
for you — frees your mind to do nothing
more than add two simple numbers.

[5.] Never. No wonder you save so much
time — avoid so many of the old errors!

6. If you didn't answer "yes," don't go on
until you've gone over the preceding
material & <u>do</u> understand it thoroughly.

MULTIPLE-COLUMN PROBLEMS

Now, how do you use this new method when you come
across a problem in everyday addition — a common
task like adding several <u>four-column</u> figures, such as
bills? I'll show you.

Remember I told you that you'd add, subtract, multiply <u>from left to right,</u> because that was the way that
made the most sense? This is the way we'll work with
the figures in multiple-column addition, for two very
good reasons: first, in this way we learn what we want
to know more quickly; second, & more important, it's
much easier!

If you're sitting at your desk with a pile of bills in
front of you — $13.41 owed to the telephone company,
a $9.26 electric bill, the mortgage payment of $85.00,
gas charges of $4.85, $26.98 for that new hat, $38.55 to
the grocery, and a pair of new tires that are going to
cost you $53.66 — the right-hand figures, the cents,
are the least of your immediate worries. What you
want to know is how many <u>dollars</u> all of that will cost
you this month.

For example, look at the problem on page 32:

1	3	.	4	1	telephone
	9	.	2	6	electricity
8	5	.	0	0	mortgage
	4	.	8	5	gas
2	6	.	9	8	hat
3	8	.	5	5	groceries
5	3	.	6	6	tires

Work the problem out this way — first, add the left-hand (tens-of-dollars) column, using the dot-method that you mastered in the first part of this chapter:

1

8

    (Nine, dot-one, four,
· 2   nine and then write
      that nineteen at the bottom.)

3

5

19

Then move to the right, over to the next — the "dollars" column — and do the same thing — completely independent of the first column:

```
1 3
  ·9
8 5      (Dot-two, seven, dot-one,
  ·4       seven, dot-five, eight, and
           then 38 at the bottom.)
2 6
3 ·8
5 3
1 9 8
3
```

Did you see where I placed the 3 of that 38? Under the 9 of the first column. Where else could it have gone, since the 8 must go directly under the column you just added? That's the great thing about working from left to right — you can't misplace digits. You just can't miss!

So remember this:

Whenever you add a multiple-digit column of figures, as in this example, this is what will happen. When you finish adding each column, you're going to end up with a number of dots and a single digit (in this case you end up with three dots and an 8). Write that digit (8) directly under the column you have just added. Then place the total of the dots (3 in this example) one column to the left of the column you've just added (in this case, under the 9).

The next step in our sample problem is column three:

```
    1 3 4
      9 2
    8 5 0        (Six, dot-four, dot-three,
      4 ·8          eight, dot-four, 34.)
    2 6 ·9
    3 8 5
    5 3 ·6
  1 9 8 4
    3 3
```

Remember to place the 4 directly under the column you've just added. Then count the dots, and place the 3 in the first available space to the left.

And, finally, column four, last <u>and</u> least:

```
    1 3 4 1
      9 2 6
    8 5 0 0       (Seven, dot-two, dot-
      4 8 ·5         zero, five, dot-one,
    2 6 9 ·8         31.)
    3 8 5 5
    5 3 6 ·6
  1 9 8 4 1
    3 3 3
```

Place the 1 under the column you've just added. Count up the dots (3), & place one space to the left.

So you see, first I simplified the adding of a single column for you. And now I've simplified the adding of multiple-column problems by breaking them into a series of simple, one-column problems.

Now, all that remains is to add those bottom two lines, which are your totals of all the columns.

Don't forget: you work from left to right, and you don't do any carrying at all. But before writing down each digit, sneak a peek at the next pair of digits to the right. If they add to more than 9, add 1 to the digit you're about to record. With your new proficiency at combining digits, you shouldn't require more than a glance to determine whether or not to add one. Here's how this works in the sample problem:

```
1 9 8 4 1
  3 3 3
2 3 1 7 1
```

The first column adds to 1, but a glance at its neighboring 9 and 3 indicates that we must add 1, to make it 2.

Now go to the 9 and 3. This gives us what looks like 2 at first glance, but once again the right-hand neighboring column exceeds 10. So record a 3.

The third column — 8 and 3 — gives a 1. And since the next column to the right equals less than 10, we simply record the 1.

And then we see that 4 and 3 are 7, and the right-hand column simply equals 1.

So the answer is simple: $231.71 (although paying all those bills might prove a little bit more difficult!).

LET'S HAVE A LITTLE MORE DRILL!

Here are a few problems to increase your ability at adding those bottom two lines of multiple-column additions.

Work from left to right, remembering always to sneak a peek at the column neighboring to the right, and determining whether a unit has to be added to the digit you're about to record.

DRILL IN LEFT-TO-RIGHT ADDITION

1.
```
1 3 3 7 6
  2 4 2
---------
1 5 7 9 6
```

2.
```
2 4 8 7 9
    6 3 4
---------
3 1 2 1 9
```

3.
```
1 2 4 7 8
    3 0 3
---------
```

4.
```
3 6 9 1 2
    2 4 7
---------
```

5.
```
5 5 5 5 5
    5 5 5
---------
```

6.
```
2 4 9 1 3
    2 3 3
---------
```

7.
```
3 1 6 8 9
    3 4 1
---------
```

8.
```
1 7 8 4 1
    1 6 4
---------
```

9.
```
4 4 7 7 1
    4 4 4
---------
```

10.
```
  31943
-   116
───────
```

11.
```
  41623
-   253
───────
```

12.
```
  17637
-   758
───────
```

13.
```
  26849
-   477
───────
```

14.
```
  26634
-   578
───────
```

15.
```
  25721
-   443
───────
```

Your answer to that very last problem should be 30,151, not 20,151. Do you see why?

When you looked at the second (5 and 4) column to determine whether to add a unit to the 2 of the first column, you saw a combination totaling less than 10, and assumed that no increase was required. But then you progressed a column to the right and peeked at 7 and 4; then you realized that by adding a unit to the second-column 9, you brought it to 10, so you should have increased the value of that first-column 2. If you kept your head and didn't panic, you drew a tail onto the 2 you had already written — 3.

It's a good idea to keep an eye out for traps such as this one. Whenever you see a 9, it might pay to be a little suspicious — and it can't hurt to let your eyes roam a teeny bit further to the right.

OR, LEARN THIS BONUS SIMPLIFIER!

Are you having trouble grasping the sneak-a-peek technique of concluding addition problems? When you tried the sample problems did you continually forget to sneak that peek?

Well, I'm not going to tell you to forget about getting this technique down pat, because it's going to help you enormously in many, many instances. Most instances, in fact. So practice it. Drill. Then practice some more. Go back and read these pages again, and then do the same problems again. And then, when you've completely mastered the sneak-a-peek technique, I'll show you another new method of adding short columns from left to right.

THE UNDERLINE

Okay. All set? Here's the new method. It involves

a brand-new device that qualifies as mathematical shorthand in the same way that the <u>dot</u> does — it's a simple "symbol" that can be as useful in <u>adding short columns</u> (two or three numbers) as the <u>dot</u> is in adding long ones — it's the <u>underline.</u> The <u>dot</u> = 10, and the <u>underline</u> = +1.

That's all! Whenever you <u>underline</u> a number, you increase its value by 1.   7̲ = 8.   4̲ = 5.   9̲ = 10. It's as simple as that. Watch:

```
    1 9 9 4 1
      3 3 3
    1̲ 2̲ 2 7 1  —  23271
```

Could anything be simpler? The first (left) column = 1.   The second column — 9 + 3 = 12.   That's over 9, so <u>underline the answer in the first column,</u> automatically increasing the 1 to 2, and record the 2 of the 12 in the second column. The <u>underline automatically</u> takes care of raising the first digit by 1!

Continue just like that to the end of the problem, and you've got 1̲ 2̲ 2 7 1.   Since the <u>underline</u> increases the value of a number by 1, that <u>means</u> 2 3 2 7 1.

Of course in this particular problem the sneak-a-peek technique would have been even faster than the <u>underline</u> technique; that's why I insisted that you master it. But I intentionally selected a simple example in this explanation, so that you could see the new gimmick clearly. And when you come up against a tricky problem that can trap you with all kinds of 9's, your use of the <u>underline</u> will be the fastest, best move you can make. For example:

```
    4 6 8 3 2
  +   3 2 8
    4 9
```

The first two columns in this one aren't any trouble at all . . . but take a look at what happens next:

```
    4 6 8 3 2
      3 2 8
    4 9 0
```

In the third column of the problem, 8 + 2 = 10; so you record the 0 and underline the 9 in the preceding column. The underline turns that 9 into a 10, though . . . so you've got to back up still another column:

```
    4 6 8 3 2
      3 2 8
    4 9 0
```

and turn that 4 into a 5 by underlining it. Now the rest is smooth sailing; finish up quickly, and you've got

```
    4 6 8 3 2
      3 2 8
    4 9 0 1 2  —  50112
```

Whenever you underline a 9, you must also underline the preceding digit.

That should give you some indication of how the underline can simplify many addition problems. You're

not required to be constantly looking ahead of what
you're doing, as you are with the sneak-a-peek technique (even if just a <u>bit</u> ahead, and just for a split second); you write down each partial sum immediately, and
adjust it later with the <u>underline.</u> Later in this book,
when we get into multiplication, you'll see some even
more dramatic uses of the <u>underline</u> that can cut your
work literally in half.

You can even push the <u>underline</u> a step further. <u>Two</u>
steps further. You increase a number by 1 when you
<u>underline</u> it. . .and you increase a number by <u>two</u> when
you underline it <u>twice.</u> <u>6</u> = 8. And you increase the
value of a number by <u>three</u> when you <u>underline</u> it <u>three</u>
times! <u>4</u> = 7.

And all that comes in mighty handy when you come
across a problem like this:

```
2  7  9  5
4 ·6 ·5  0
1 ·8 ·8 ·6
7  1  2  1  —  9 3 3 1
```

Note those dots in there! Those are the dots that
you use to keep track of the tens as you add a column
of numbers. In the second column — 7 + 6 + 8 — the
6 brings you past 10, so you place a dot beside it and
continue adding, with the 3; the 8 brings you past 10
once again, so you record a dot and write down 1 at the
bottom of the column.

Note that wherever a column produced <u>two</u> dots, the
preceding answer digit was underlined <u>twice.</u> And just
one dot meant just one <u>underline</u> for the preceding column's answer digit.

DRILL IN UNDERLINES

The rule in left-to-right addition of short columns is this:

Add columns from left to right, recording the sum of each column immediately. But if the sum of any column equals or exceeds 10, record the right-hand digit of that sum beneath the column and underline the answer digit immediately to the left — one underline for every unit of the sum's left-hand digit.

```
   3 7
  +4 8
  ─────
   7̲ 5
```

The first thing you did to solve this addition problem was to add the left-hand column — 3 + 4 = 7 — and record the 7 beneath the column.

The second step was to combine the digits in the second column.   7 + 8 = 15 . . . so you recorded the 5 (the right-hand digit of the 15) beneath the column, and simply underlined the 7 (which you had recorded as the sum of the column to the left), increasing its value to 8. The correct answer is 85.

Before you try another drill, let's go over one last problem step by step — a problem which involves everything you've learned about left-to-right addition:

```
   3 6 4
   2 7 3      "Three . . . five . . . six."
   1̲ 9̲ 6̲        Write down 6.
   ─────
       6
```

That's what you think as you add the left-hand column.

```
3  6  4     Six . . . dot-three . . . dot-two.
2 ·7  3     Write down 2, underline 6 twice.
1 ·9  6
6  2
=
```

The second column is a little more complex. Twice your subtotal exceeded 10, so twice you made a dot and carried on with just the right-hand digit of the subtotal. So you wrote in the 2, and adjusted the first column's answer digit by giving it two underlines. One underline for each dot.

```
3  6  4     Four . . . seven. . . dot-three.
2 ·7  3     Write down 3, and underline the 2.
1 ·9 ·6
6  2  3  —  8 3 3
=  _
```

For the third column, you added, recording just one dot for exceeding 10. You wrote down the 3, and underlined the preceding column's answer digit once to compensate for the single dot.   6 2 3 = 8 3 3, the correct answer.

If you understand this problem's solution completely, and if you also can use the sneak-a-peek technique on two-row additions — then you're with me so far.

BUILDING SPEED IN MULTIPLE-
COLUMN ADDITION

Now then, if you can see that every multiple-column addition problem can be broken down into a series of single-column problems — all that remains is to gain proficiency at multiple-column addition through practice. So here are some problems in:

TWO-COLUMN ADDITION

1.	3 4
	·8 ·7
	3 8
	·6 ·6
	7 ·8

2 7 3
3
3 0 3

2.	6 8
	7 8
	8 3
	4 9
	5 4

3.	2 2
	6 9
	6 6
	9 9
	3 3

4.	6 5
	9 6
	4 5
	8 8
	6 9

5.	9 1
	4 4
	1 8
	7 7
	<u>8 9</u>

6.	4 7
	6 3
	2 1
	9 9
	<u>8 5</u>

7.	9 2
	1 1
	6 8
	8 7
	<u>8 8</u>

8.	5 6
	6 5
	7 7
	8 8
	<u>7 4</u>

9.	1 9
	8 3
	3 1
	3 8
	<u>6 7</u>

10.	4 7
	4 8
	2 5
	1 1
	<u>9 9</u>

THREE-COLUMN ADDITION

1.
```
    4 8 1
    5 ·9 1
   ·2 ·8 1
    8 ·8 ·7
   ·3 2 1
  ─────────
  2 2 5 1
    3 1
  ─────────
  2 5 6 1
```

2.
```
  5 6 6
  1 8 6
  1 0 0
  8 9 9
  7 6 0
  ─────
```

3.
```
  2 9 8
  6 0 2
  7 9 9
  9 8 8
    4 1
  ─────
```

4.
```
  7 4 2
  7 8 8
  9 4 3
  5 6 5
  6 7 7
  ─────
```

5.
```
  7 7 9
  6 6 0
  3 8 7
  4 3 3
  7 8 8
  ─────
```

6.
```
  4 2 9
  7 3 8
  3 5 5
  3 5 6
  9 4 7
  ─────
```

7.
```
  8 5 6
  7 5 6
  3 0 8
  2 9 4
    6 7
  ─────
```

8.
```
  8 6 7
  7 6 8
  8 8 7
  6 6 8
  7 8 6
  ─────
```

9.	4 2 9	10.	4 1 7
	9 8 7		2 9 1
	7 4 6		4 4 2
	6 3 8		6 6 8
	8 8 1		8 4 3

FOUR-COLUMN ADDITION

1.   4 8 5 0
  ·8 ·5 ·9 8
  6 ·8 5 ·9
 ·8 7 ·5 ·9
 ·5 ·4 4 ·5
3 1 2 8 1
  3 2 3
3 4, 5 1 1

2.	3 7 9 3	3.	6 2 7 7	4.	8 8 8 8
	5 5 8 8		6 0 0 0		9 9 9
	6 8 5 9		6 8 5 9		4 8 9 1
	9 0 0 1		5 4 4 5		6 7 9 9
	8 7 5 6		6 7 8 8		7 6 0 7

5.	9 1 5 6	6.	2 9 5 8	7.	8 1 8 2
	1 2 8 7		4 3 7 2		1 9 1 9
	3 8 8 2		3 8 8 7		3 4 4 9
	9 9 8 8		6 1 5 1		5 4 4 0
	7 7 9 9		4 7 0 9		3 6 7 2

8.	1 2 3 4	9.	4 3 4 4	10.	7 8 8 0
	8 7 6 5		6 4 5 4		9 5 6 4
	9 1 0 1		4 7 4 8		8 8 9 7
	1 2 1 1		5 9 4		5 7 8 6
	3 1 4 9		5 1 5 2		9 9 2 8

By this time, I'm sure, you're convinced that you are able to add more accurately and quickly than you ever could before. But here's a chance to prove it to yourself even more convincingly, and at the same time give yourself still more practice at your new ability.

Work out the problems on page 50 using the streamlining methods that I've shown you in this chapter, and then check your answers with the correct ones in the back of this book.

YOUR FINAL EXAM IN LIGHTNING ADDITION

1.	8	2.	4 1	3.	6 6 6
	5		1 2		6 5 8
	7		9 9		3 0 0
	6		7 6		7 0
	4				5 4 1
	3				2 2 1
	3				

4.	3 6 3,7 8 9.4 5	5.	2 7.8 5	6.	9
	4 4,0 0 0.0 1		5 5.0 9		9
	9 9 7,6 8 5.0 0		1 1.9 8		8
	3 7.8 8		4 4.8 7		8
			5 5.6 2		7
			2 2.0 1		7
			4 5.4 7		6
			3 5.9 9		6
			8 8.2 4		5
			3 4.9 5		5
			9 5.9 9		4
			1 0.0 0		4
			6 5.2 9		3
			3 3.4 4		3
					2
					2
					1
					1

7.	100,000	8.	47	9.	45,988
	10,000		65		22,645
	1,000		88		34,921
	999		89		16,667
	900,001		98		56,117
			86		69,012
			65		83,388
			49		27,722
			38		50,094
			28		58,852
			77		33,848
			74		
			66		

10.	9623	11.	365	12.	14.6722
	2461		609		68.2218
	4324		765		80.927
	7189		982		45.8734
			430		8.7
			667		23.2323
			229		22.9229
			277		27.7227
			886		33.3333
			774		
			554		
			998		
			736		
			872		

How To Shift Addition Into High Gear; Making Lightning-Quick Estimates; And Mental Math

Aside from all the time that modern methods slash away from work on addition, you can — in a tremendous number of special cases — reduce your work still more, by using one of these amazing short-cut devices. Don't lose out when paper isn't available . . . make estimates mentally, in a flash!

"There's more here, sir. . .than meets the eye."
— John Galsworthy, "The Man of Property."

The dot, the underline, the sneak-a-peek technique . . . the entire method of long addition which you've just learned will become one of the most useful lessons of your life. The time you continue to spend drilling, practicing, and testing yourself isn't time wasted; indeed, every minute you devote to mastery of this method will come back to you tenfold in time saved, in increased accuracy, in greater confidence in your own ability.

And just because you've been such a good student, I'm going to tell you about a few useful techniques for doing addition when you need a fast estimate, or when paper isn't available!

How often have you been confronted with the seemingly hopeless task of adding a string of numbers all in your head?

For example, you're in the supermarket, and you want to be sure, as you walk around filling the cart, that you won't take more products off the shelves than you can pay for out-of-pocket.

Or your boss comes to you with a sales report, and he asks you to comment — on the spot — on the latest totals.

Or while you're working on the monthly budget, your daughter asks if there'll be enough extra for a new prom gown.

How do you come up with the right figures — fast — without reaching for a pencil?

Here are a few "special" gimmicks which will enable you to make rapid estimates mentally. Enable you to solve many addition problems to whatever degree of accuracy you wish, without ever putting a pen to paper.

And you'll be able to utilize these mental gimmicks far more effectively because of the practice you had in the last chapter — practice which enabled you to master my streamlined method of addition.

THE FIRST SECRET: DOT = 10; FINGER = DOT!

Let's say that next week you're watching a Little League game. You glance up at the scoreboard, and you see this line score:

Your Son's Team	4	6	9	5	3	8	2
The Bad Guys		7	2	4	3	8	9	1

Who won the game? Well, if you had a piece of paper, you'd do it this way:

Your Team	Their Team
4	7
·6	2
9	·4
·5	3
3	·8
·8	·9
2	1
3 7	3 4

So your son's a winner. But you wouldn't know it if you didn't have a pencil and paper with you, unless you know the secret formula <u>finger = dot</u>! Look at the scoreboard again, and add it this way:

Your Son's Team	4 6 9 5 3 8 2
The Bad Guys	7 2 4 3 8 9 1

Now start to add your son's score on your fingers. 4 + 6 = finger-0. Then 9. Then second-<u>finger</u>-4. Then 7. Then third-<u>finger</u>-5. Then 7 again.

You have raised three fingers, and have 7 left over. So his team scored 37.

Now let's do the bad guys' score. 7 + 2 = 9. Then first-finger-3. Then 6. Then second-finger-4. Then third-finger-3. Then 4.

You have raised three fingers again, but have only 4 left over (34). Your side won. Who ever said that counting on your fingers wasn't any good?

Do you understand what I did? Finger-figuring is exactly the same as the method of adding columns with dots. But instead of making a dot each time you reach 10 or higher, you stick out a finger. And with your own ten fingers, you can count to 100 or 1,000, as we'll see later in this chapter.

Now for a little practice. Add these columns mentally, using your fingers the same way you'd use dots on paper.

DRILL IN MENTAL ADDITION — FINGER METHOD

1.	4	2.	3
	9		7
	2		6
	6		4
	3		9
	8		2
	1		8

3.	4	4.	6	5.	5	6.	6
	9		2		8		4
	9		9		8		3
	9		4		5		7
	3		7		5		7
	2		6		8		3
	7		6		8		5

[7.] 9	[8.] 8	[9.] 4	[10.] 1
2	7	3	2
8	6	4	9
3	7	9	3
7	8	8	4
4	7	7	8
6	6	2	6

SECOND SECRET: THE ROUND-OFF

Here's a tip on rapid estimating that will be useful in countless situations, from shopping sprees to motor trips.

Let's say you're planning a scenic auto tour of the Southwest. You pull out the trusty atlas and plot a route from your house in Bigpine to your uncle's rancho in Sweetwater. You trace the tentative path of your trip with a fingertip, and it looks like this:

Bigpine — Los Angeles	261 (miles)
Los Angeles — Phoenix	394
Phoenix — Tucson	122
Tucson — El Paso	347
El Paso — Van Horn	120
Van Horn — Big Spring	222
Big Spring — Sweetwater	74

That's what your fingertip traced. But with this second short cut, each time you come to a new number, round off that number to the nearest hundred in your mind, and add it to a running subtotal. Like this:

300 (+400) = 700 (+100) = 800 (+300) = 1100 (+100) = 1200 (+200) = 1400 (+100) = 1,500 total miles.

And you did all that rounding off and adding up in your head, as quickly as your finger traced its path. And by the time it had reached Sweetwater you knew that the distance you had to travel was about 1,500 miles.

Actually, it's 1,540 miles. The round-off estimate in this particular case was less than 3% off! Pretty close, isn't it, for a mental estimate?

Remember that whenever the number is 50 or more, 150 or more, 250 or more, 350 or more, round it off to the next highest 100. If the number is 49 or less, 149 or less, 249 or less, and so on, round it off to the next lowest 100. For example, try this problem:

```
    4 7 3
    1 4 9
    8 2 7
    5 8 0
    2 9 2
      4 7
    3 2 9
    6 6 4
```

You should have figured as follows: 5 (hundred) + 1 (hundred) make 6 (hundred). Six and 8 are 14, and 6 are 20, and 3 are 23. (The 47 is under 50, so it isn't counted at all. But, glancing at the next number, 329, you should have considered the 329 as 4, not 3, because 329 and 47 are obviously more than 350.)

So — you're up to 23 and 4 are 27, and 7 are 34, or 3400. Even if you hadn't thought of utilizing that 47, you would have mentally estimated 3300. Either way you're pretty close to the actual total of 3361.

What about another occasion when you might find the round-off estimating method useful? Well, walk through the supermarket, dropping item after item into your shopping cart — a loaf of bread marked 26¢ (think 30). A

49¢ can of juice (think 50). Pet food 33¢ (think 30). And
so on, until you've either completed your shopping list
. . . or depleted your shopping cash.

You can make the round-off as accurate as you care
to, if you're willing to put in the extra effort. If, for
example, you wanted to estimate the cost of materials
required to build a yacht, and you had been quoted prices
of $1,224.38 for lumber, $439.60 for paint, $694.16 for
hardware, $708.42 for glass, and $1,483.09 for assorted
fittings, you might be satisfied with 1200 + 400 + 700 +
700 + 1500 = $4,500.

Or, if your budget is really tight, you might want to
take the extra trouble of rounding off to nearest 25's —
1225 + 450 + 700 + 700 + 1475 = $4,550.

Either way, you wouldn't be very far from the exact
cost — $4,549.65.

The round-off method of mental estimating works
very well in combination with the finger method of keeping track of 10's. (I'll bet you already thought of that.)

For example, consider this problem of estimating
the number of students in the eleventh grade at Bridge-
ton High School:

> Class 111 — 57 students
>
> Class 112 — 62 students
>
> Class 113 — 55 students
>
> Class 114 — 73 students
>
> Class 115 — 68 students

When you work on this type of problem, just do this:

1. Drop the zeros from the rounded off num-
    bers (57 becomes 60, but you count it on
    your fingers as though it were 6 — just as
    I dropped the two zeros in the example on
    page 57).

2. Then, when you get the final answer, simply put back that zero. (Your final finger count of 32 gets an extra zero, and becomes 320.)

Here's how the actual finger-counting is done:

Start with 6. Then first-finger-2. Then 8. Then second-finger-5. Then third-finger-2.

Three fingers — equals 32. Now, replace the zero, and you've got an estimated 320 students in the eleventh grade. Only 5 away from the actual count of 315.

Now you try a bit of estimating, with the use of mental round-off, just to see how simple — and how surprisingly accurate — it really is:

DRILL IN MENTAL ADDITION (ESTIMATING) — ROUND-OFF METHOD

1.	2.
4 9	3 2
7 3	8 8
8 6	9 6
3 4	6 9
2 9	3 7
4 3	4 8
7 6	8 1
8 8	3 3
2 1	2 9
3 4	6 2

3.	27	4.	69	5.	48	6.	18
	81		97		89		28
	64		81		93		38
	93		24		21		48
	75		36		47		58
	81		44		74		12
	14		91		88		22
	33		80		26		32
	94		47		43		42
	28		83		41		52

7.	49	8.	87	9.	89	10.	27
	82		61		93		64
	63		78		76		48
	77		80		44		89
	64		19		81		68
	48		20		27		33
	44		58		35		21
	39		79		63		47
	22		22		68		39
	17		38		82		84

THIRD SECRET: MENTAL ADDITION
BY PIECE-WORK

It should be obvious to you now that one of the cardinal rules of miracle mathematics is to — eliminate confusion by exchanging a complicated procedure for a series of simple procedures.

If you can get the correct answer by taking two or three short steps, why risk everything on one big step, especially one that might be too big?

The tip that I'm about to describe to you is the perfect example of that rule. Doing an addition problem by piece-work is nothing more — or less — revolutionary than taking one step at a time . . . each step short and simple, but becoming part of a big trip.

For example, how much is 42,378 + 9,424? Is that too difficult to work out mentally? Well, try it this way:

Simply break down the 9,424 to the easy-to-add numbers 9,000 . . . 400 . . . 20 . . . and 4.

Now the problem goes like this:

How much is
42,378 + 9,000?

(Not so difficult now, is it? Add the 9(000) to 42(378), to get 51,378.)

Now, how much is
51,378 + 400?

(Easy; add the 4(00) to the 3(78) to get 51,778.)

And how much is
51,778 + 20?

(No problem here; 20 to 51,778 is 51,798.)

Finally, how much is
51,798 + 4?

(Adding 4 to 51,798 gives you the final answer· 51,802.)

Now you have it! You solve the problem one step at a time — piece-work — starting on the left, where the important numbers are. The first estimate you get is the most important figure you need. And you don't bother to figure any further than the step which gives you as accurate an answer as you want for that particular problem.

Here's one more example to show you what a simple and useful idea this is. To add 37,243 + 8,738 mentally, think it like this:

$$37,243 + 8,000 = 45,243$$
$$45,243 + 700 = 45,943$$
$$45,943 + 30 = 45,973$$
$$45,973 + 8 = 45,981 \text{ (final, and correct, total).}$$

Even the words show you exactly where to add each digit — eight thousand is naturally combined with thirty-seven thousand. And hundreds go to hundreds, and tens to tens, and units to units.

This piece-work method makes addition of large numbers child's play, because it reduces each problem to a series of simple calculations — of combining one pair of digits.

What's more, carving up the job in this way provides an automatic system of rapid estimating, with the accuracy of the estimate increased step by step. For example, if you're looking for a movie camera and projector, and you have only $150 to spend, you don't have to figure beyond 7 and 9 when you see a $75.00 camera and a $99.50 projector.

Now prove to yourself how amazingly simple this piece-work method makes mental addition. Don't use a pencil, but solve mentally the problems in this

DRILL IN MENTAL ADDITION — PIECE-WORK METHOD

[1.] 4,623 + 346 =   [2.] 86,311 + 13,077 =

[3.] $38.75 + $5.98 =   [4.] 8,327 + 1,629 =

[5.] 49,982 + 63,001 =   [6.] 2,398 + 403 =

[7.] $29.98 + $77.11 =   [8.] 78 + 83.12 =

[9.] 432 + 888 =   [10.] $48.95 + $1.05 =

FOURTH SECRET: WHEN THE CHIPS ARE DOWN — THE ELEVATOR METHOD OF ADDING

This is it. One day you'll run into a long-addition problem, and there'll be no getting away from it — you'll want to know the exact answer to that problem, and there won't be a scrap of paper or a burnt cork within miles.

I'm going to show you just what to do when that happens. It can be as sure a solution as the one you'd get with pen and paper, but it won't be as lightning-fast as round-off estimating. It will do right well in a pinch, however.

In fact, with practice, you can be adding long columns to the amazement of all who behold you in the office, at parties, and at home.

```
Watch:   4 3 8
         2 7 4
         9 6 1
         8 8 3
         7 2 4
```

That problem can just as well represent the number of times Sandy Koufax struck out your five favorite Giants, or the prices of your lunches for the week, or anything at all.

But let's get going; no pen and paper now.

To start, put your finger beside the 4 in the upper left-hand corner of the problem — the top of the first column. Moving your finger slowly down the column, adding as you go; say after me: 6, 15, 23, 30.

(You could have used the finger method to keep track of the tens as you added, but you wouldn't be able to

continue using those fingers from this point on. Besides, I want to spell this procedure out completely this
time, just to be sure you follow what I'm doing.)

All right; you're at the bottom of the left-hand column, and you've added up to 30. Now — tack on the
digit immediately to the right of the last digit you added,
like this:

The last digit your finger crossed was the 7 at the
bottom of the first column, and the digit to its right is
the 2 at the bottom of the second column, right?

So tack the 2 onto the 30, resulting in 302. Not 32;
that would be adding the 2 to the 30. I said tack it on
— 302.

Once that's done, move your finger slowly up the
second column, adding as it crosses each number, from
302 upward — 310, 316, 323, 326.

That's two columns down; one to go. To the 326,
tack on the digit to the right of the last digit you added.
The last digit you added was the 3 at the top of the second column; the digit to its right is the 8 at the top of
the third column. So tack that 8 onto the 326 — that
gives you 3268.

Now move your finger down that final column, adding
to 3268 — 3272, 3273, 3276, and 3280! Koufax fanned
that quintet of batters a grand total of 3,280 times!

That solution involved a lot of big numbers, but there
really wasn't any way of avoiding it, was there? At
least you were only adding one little number at a time.
And you'll find that it helps to say each subtotal aloud
as you go along: thirty-two-sixty-eight, thirty-two-
seventy-two, thirty-two-seventy-three. It helps.

Pretend the chips are down. Remember the technique
of adding down one column and up the next like an elevator, tacking the first digit of each column on to the
subtotal up to that point.

If you will just try the idea, perhaps you will be as
thrilled with it as I am. Practice it and learn it —

you'll be glad you did.

Here's another example:

```
7 3 1
4 8 6
9 2 3
5 4 2
6 2 3
```

Start at the upper left, the 7, and say to yourself aloud: "Seven and 4 is 11, and 9 is 20, and 5 is 25, and 6 is 31." Tack the 2 (bottom digit of second column) onto the 31, saying, "Three twelve." Now continue going up the second column.

312, 316, 318, 326, 329. Tack the 1 (top digit of third column) onto the 329, saying, "Thirty-two, ninety-one." Now continue down the third column.

3291, 3297, 3300, 3302, 3305. The correct total is 3305.

Now, do not continue reading until you try the elevator method on these columns of numbers:

DRILL IN MENTAL ADDITION —
ELEVATOR METHOD

1.		2.		3.	
	3 6 1		4 7 1		3 3 7
	4 8 3		6 3 9		6 2 8
	9 2 2		7 2 7		8 6 2
	6 4 7		8 1 6		9 4 4
	8 2 8		1 4 3		3 1 1

4.	8 1 3	5.	5 1 9	6.	4 1 4
	3 5 5		9 5 6		8 8 1
	8 8 3		6 4 3		7 2 3
	6 0 4		7 8 2		3 4 1
	7 2 0		6 2 1		3 8 3

7.	9 2 3	8.	4 4 0	9.	4 9 9
	4 3 8		9 1 6		8 1 4
	7 6 8		3 2 7		1 3 4
	8 4 1		5 2 3		6 4 2
	1 1 7		2 3 2		6 3 0

10.	2, 6 3 4
	6, 0 1 8
	1, 8 3 0
	3 4 1
	2, 0 6 1

NOW LET'S SUM IT ALL UP!

I'd be willing to bet, right now, that as you solved the problems in these last few drills you really surprised yourself with your ability to perform addition in you head.

These "gimmicks" can produce some really dramatic results, but their real worth is in cutting down your work whenever you must get an answer fast to business, financial, and dozens of other problems that come up daily.

To do this, you must be able to look at an addition problem and quickly determine which of the tricks in your repertoire will best do the job.

Let's briefly review the techniques of mental addition you've learned in these last pages, and then I'll put you to a real test of your new skill in addition — a series of diverse problems, for each of which you'll have to select the technique for calculating your answer.

1. The Finger Method. Use fingers just as you'd use dots in adding a column on paper. Every time you reach ten or higher, stick out a finger and continue with the right-hand digit of the partial sum.

Do an example: $4 + 9 + 8 =$ first-finger-3. Then second-finger-1. Then 21.

2. The Round-Off Method. Round off each number in the series to the nearest ten, or hundred, or thousand, and add the rounded-off numbers with the finger method.

Do an example: When you add $378 + 226 + 761 + 499 + 338$, you round them off to $400 + 200 + 800 + 500 + 300$ — and then forget the zeros and finger-add 6. Then first-finger-4. Then 9. Then second-finger-2. That's 22; replace the two zeros, which gives you 2,200. Pretty close!

3. The Piece-Work Method. Add the digits of the first number to the next number — first by thousands, then hundreds, then tens, then units.

Do an example: $23,579 + 4,724$ equals 27,579 plus 700; which equals 28,279; plus 20, which equals 28,299; plus 4, which equals 28,303.

4. The Elevator Method. Add the digits of the first column on the left. Then to their total tack on the bottom digit of the second column, continue adding upward. Then tack on the top digit of the third column to the total you reach at the top. Continue through the problem, column by column, in that manner.

Do an example:

    3 6 8 5
    2 8 7 6
    5 3 3 8
    9 2 2 1
    8 5 4 1

Add the first column, starting at the top and working down in this way: 5, 10, 19, 27.

Then tack on the 5 at the bottom of the second column to get 275.

Then add the second column, working upward: 277, 280, 288, 294.

Then tack on the 8 at the top of the third column to get 2948.

Then add the third column, working down: 2955, 2958, 2960, 2964.

Then tack on the 1 at the bottom of the fourth column to get 29641.

And then add that fourth column, working upward: 29642, 29650, 29656, 29661.

The answer is 29661.

(Remember to say & repeat the numbers to yourself as you work. This will assure that you do not forget the numbers you're working with.)

NOW PUT THEM TO WORK

Is each of these methods clear to you? Do you understand when each is especially useful?

The finger method will serve you well when you have to add a long string of single digits.

When a quick estimate will suffice, utilize the round-off method.

The piece-work method is great for adding one large number to another large number — in seconds.

And the elevator method shines whenever you just have to add a huge series of big numbers without pencil & paper.

Which method, or methods, will you choose for each of the problems in this

FINAL DRILL IN MENTAL ADDITION

1.	2 4 , 8 2 1	2.	9	3.	2 6
	+ 3 , 2 6 8		3		4 3
			4		3 7
			2		4 8
			6		7 2
			7		
			8		
			3		
			4		
			5		

4.	8 4 3	5.	3 , 2 5 9	6.	$3 7 . 5 0
	2 7 9		+1 , 8 3 4		4 2 . 9 5
	6 4 1				6 6 . 5 8
	4 2 8				1 3 . 7 5
	6 4 9				

7.	8	8.	5 6 1	9.	8 1
	5		3 8 7		5 4
	4		7 4 9		3 6
	3		3 3 6		7 2
	2		8 1 8		6 3
	9				1 8
	1				9 0
	4				
	7				
	7				

10. $246,817.37
    +   29.98

11. $419.00
    +62.95

12.   3 6 5
       4 8 1
       8 7 6
       8 4 9
       3 9 2
       4 7 8
       8 6 2
       9 1 8
       4 4 7

Mathematical Miracle Number Two—How To Subtract Without Borrowing

This chapter exposes the only difficult part about ordinary subtraction, and shows you how to eliminate it completely. Working from left to right, you'll be able to utilize the One-Second Slash, a device of mathematical shorthand that enables you to subtract perfectly nearly as quickly as you can write down the figures.

"Neither a borrower nor a lender be."

— William Shakespeare, "Hamlet."

Those words may be excellent advice in affairs of economics; but anyone who remained true to them while subtracting must reach an answer that would be false to any man. Borrowing is as vital to the mathematical operation of subtracting as the national debt is to our economy. Without it, 17 couldn't be subtracted from 23, and the answer to 45 minus 6 would be incalculable.

Yet borrowing is just exactly where most people have the most trouble, where they go wrong in subtraction.

What is the reason for this universal difficulty?
Simple. Borrowing is the one step in every subtraction
problem that — until discovery of the modern streamlining technique I'm about to show you — necessitated
your juggling different operations in your mind at exactly the same moment.

For example, look at this simple problem in everyday subtraction:

$$\begin{array}{r} 4\ 5 \\ -\ \underline{1\ 9} \end{array}$$

Let's examine the conventional, old-fashioned method of solving it.

With the old-fashioned method you begin at the right,
and then work backwards, to the left, so that the most
meaningful part of your answer will become evident to
you last of all. You begin with 5 minus 9 (5 — 9).

It becomes immediately obvious that you just can't
subtract 9 from 5 . . . you've got to find some way of
increasing that 5 to 15, so that your subtraction problem will work. You've got to "borrow" 10 from the 10's
column; and you'll have to keep that loan in mind at the
exact time that you're subtracting 9 from 15.

Now, where does the borrowed 10 come from? You
have to take it from the 4 — the 40 — at the top of the
10's column. Then you have to remember to compensate for that loan by raising the 1 (of the 19) by 1 (or
10), & so on.

Let's review the steps that you had to go through to
solve this problem the old-fashioned way:

1.   You looked at the problem, saw the right-hand
     column of 5 minus 9 and said to yourself: 9
     can't be subtracted from 5.

2.   So you borrowed 10 from the 40 to make that
     5 — 15.

3. Then you subtracted 9 from 15, and got 6.

4. This means that your answer is something-6.
    You now know that the right-hand digit of your
    answer is 6. But you still don't know what the
    left-hand digit is.

And by the time you've learned that 45 minus 19 is
something-6, the odds are high that you've forgotten
the loan you made.

You've forgotten that you've reduced the 4 to a 3.
And no wonder — you had to keep that 4-becomes-3
fact tucked away in your mind at the very same time
that you were subtracting 9 from 15. Too often you
will forget the loan . . . most people do.

The entire procedure is just too complicated, too
tedious, too vulnerable to error and forgetfulness.
There should be a simpler way. And there is! Here's
how it works:

First, eliminate the complicated part of borrowing.
Get rid of the necessity of remembering the loan at the
very same time that you're subtracting.

And then, the simple, logical, modern procedure of
working from left to right; couple it with the streamlining principle of the One-Second Slash Method; and
you'll subtract easily, sensibly, and perfectly — almost
as quickly as you write down the figures.

WORK FROM LEFT TO RIGHT

What is this One-Second Slash Method? It's a sub-
traction-simplifier that was developed as part of a
mathematical shorthand used by bookkeepers, engineers,
and scientists who must work quickly, accurately, and
logically — from left to right — so that they can tell
instantaneously whether they're on the right track. No
use working out an entire lengthy problem if the basic
tools are wrong, and the sooner you know that your
answer is really wide of the mark, the better.

For example, suppose you drive up to a new-car showroom and ask the price of a convertible that has caught your eye. Suppose the salesman tells you that the convertible lists at $2,564, and that he'll allow you $675 for your old car.

Now, what's the first thing that you want to know:

1.   That the convertible will cost you something-9 dollars — or

2.   That you'll need nearly $2,000 to drive away with the top down.

You see? Subtracting from left to right is the sensible way:

$$
\begin{array}{r}
2\ 5\ 6\ 4 \\
-\ \ \ 6\ 7\ 5 \\
\hline
1\ 8\ 8\ 9
\end{array}
$$

Then you can read the answer: one thousand, eight hundred, eighty-nine. From left to right, just the way you say the answer.

And subtracting from left to right is the easy way to get rid of the complicated part of borrowing. Because, this way, I'll show you how to borrow from the answer! How to take the extra quantity you need from the work you've already done; make the transaction on the spot; and put it immediately out of your mind.

THE ONE-SECOND SLASH METHOD

The key to doing subtraction as quickly and perfectly as you can count is a simple mark that, with just a little practice, you will use as profitably as you now use the dot, or the underline, you learned about in the previous two chapters.

Just as you can now use the dot to streamline your addition, you'll forever eliminate inaccuracy and wasted time in subtraction by using this simple short cut symbol — the <u>slash</u>.

Here is its meaning in subtraction: <u>Slash means minus one. Whenever you draw a slash through a number, you reduce its value by one!</u>

The slash looks like this: /

And it's used like this: $\cancel{5}$ = 4; $\cancel{7}$ = 6; $\cancel{9}$ = 8.

Do you understand? When you draw a slash through an 8, like this — $\cancel{8}$, the 8 becomes a 7. Because <u>Slash = Minus One</u>. $\cancel{8}$ = 7, because / = <u>−1</u>.

Try it yourself. Write in the answers to these entries:

$\cancel{9}$ = $\cancel{8}$ = $\cancel{7}$ = $\cancel{6}$ = $\cancel{5}$ =

$\cancel{4}$ = $\cancel{3}$ = $\cancel{2}$ = $\cancel{1}$ =

USING THE SLASH

Fine. Every time you draw a slash through a number you reduce its value by one. But so what? How can that help you with the complication involved in borrowing when you subtract?

In this way: Simply combine the <u>slash</u> technique with the procedure of working from left to right, and this is what happens:

$$\begin{array}{r} 4\ 5 \\ -\ 1\ 9 \\ \hline \end{array}$$

Because you're working <u>forward</u>, start at the left:

$$\begin{array}{r} 4 \\ -\ 1 \\ \hline 3 \end{array}$$

Couldn't be simpler! Now move on to the next column. . .

$$
\begin{array}{r}
4\ 5 \\
-\ 1\ 9 \\
\hline
3\ ?
\end{array}
$$

You can't subtract 9 from 5, so you must <u>borrow</u>. But why not take what you need from your answer?

You use that <u>slash</u> to make the transfer, like this:

$$
\begin{array}{r}
4 \cdot 5 \\
-\ 1\ \ 9 \\
\hline
\not{3}\ \ 6 \\
2\ \ 6
\end{array}
$$

Simply slashing the 3 (on the bottom line) gave you the extra 10 you needed to perform the subtraction in the right-hand column. The 10 is indicated in the sample problem with, of course, a <u>dot</u>!

From there, it's a simple operation: 15 ($\cdot$5) minus 9 = 6. And the answer? Since $\not{3}$ = 2, the answer is 26. You write it right below.

Here's the procedure:

1.   Work from left to right, and

2.   Whenever it becomes necessary to subtract a larger number from a smaller one, <u>transfer 10 to the upper right-hand digit by slashing the answer-digit of the preceding column.</u>

Incidentally, please don't worry about marking up your problems with dots, underlines, or slashes. In the old-fashioned methods, you had to mark up the problems with small digits (the carryings); these were usually unrecognizable or completely forgotten. The dots and slashes are easily recognized — and save time and avoid errors.

Of course, in subtraction — after some practice — you won't have to bother putting in the dots. Once you've made the <u>slash</u> you can carry (oops!), I mean go on without carrying, and so on.

TRY IT YOURSELF

Ready to try the One-Second Slash for yourself? Remember that slashing a digit reduces its value by 1, and that each slash entitles you to increase the number at the upper right by 10. A good way to remind yourself of this is to see where the slash points.

All right, then, try this:

DRILL IN LEFT-TO-RIGHT, SLASH METHOD SUBTRACTION

1.
```
    2 ·1
  - 1  4
    ⫽  7
  (0)  7
```

2.
```
    1 6
  -   8
```

3.
```
    3 8
  - 2 9
```

4.
```
    4 2
  - 1 3
```

5.
```
    6 0
  - 1 1
```

6.
```
    1 3
  -   9
```

7.
```
    1 2
  -   9
```

8.
```
    4 7
  - 2 8
```

9.
```
    3 0
  - 2 2
```

10.
```
    6 6
  - 4 7
```

11.
```
    8 8
  - 1 9
```

[12.]	8 4	[13.]	7 6	[14.]	6 7
	− 3 5		− 6 7		− 2 9

[15.]	9 0	[16.]	4 4	[17.]	6 4
	− 3 1		− 1 5		− 2 7

[18.]	3 6	[19.]	2 4	[20.]	8 2
	− 9		− 1 5		− 2 3

Do you see how the slash took your mind off the procedure of "borrowing" — how it let you concentrate entirely on performing the individual subtracting operations?

Just as the dot in addition enables you to devote all your mental energies to adding simple digits, so the slash enables you to concentrate 100% of your brainpower on subtracting simple digits. But to become perfect at this new, easier, faster way of subtracting you need, of course, practice — so let's start picking up that practice right now.

MEMORIZE THESE "EASY-
SUBTRACTION" CHARTS

The following is a chart of all the natural subtractions that you will ever have to perform. By natural subtractions, I mean that the top number is larger than the bottom number. That you don't have to borrow from somewhere else to make the subtraction.

$9 - 9 = 0$

$9 - 8 = 1$ $8 - 8 = 0$

$9 - 7 = 2$ $8 - 7 = 1$ $7 - 7 = 0$

$9 - 6 = 3$ $8 - 6 = 2$ $7 - 6 = 1$ $6 - 6 = 0$

$9 - 5 = 4$ $8 - 5 = 3$ $7 - 5 = 2$ $6 - 5 = 1$ $5 - 5 = 0$

$9 - 4 = 5$ $8 - 4 = 4$ $7 - 4 = 3$ $6 - 4 = 2$ $5 - 4 = 1$ $4 - 4 = 0$

$9 - 3 = 6$ $8 - 3 = 5$ $7 - 3 = 4$ $6 - 3 = 3$ $5 - 3 = 2$ $4 - 3 = 1$ $3 - 3 = 0$

$9 - 2 = 7$ $8 - 2 = 6$ $7 - 2 = 5$ $6 - 2 = 4$ $5 - 2 = 3$ $4 - 2 = 2$ $3 - 2 = 1$ $2 - 2 = 0$

$9 - 1 = 8$ $8 - 1 = 7$ $7 - 1 = 6$ $6 - 1 = 5$ $5 - 1 = 4$ $4 - 1 = 3$ $3 - 1 = 2$ $2 - 1 = 1$ $1 - 1 = 0$

There are forty-five of them. I imagine you are familiar with them all right now. Make sure you can do every one of them perfectly, instantly, automatically before you go on.

Now let's look at the "un-natural" possibilities — those subtraction problems that require borrowing.

If you're well-rehearsed in using the One-Second Slash Method, you'll do the following whenever you bump into such a problem:

Draw a slash through the digit of the answer beneath the preceding column.

Then all you've got to know — on sight, preferably — are the forty-five possibilities on page 81 (written here with dots, which is how they would look in an actual problem):

								·0 − 1 = 9
							·1 − 2 = 9	·0 − 2 = 8
						·2 − 3 = 9	·1 − 3 = 8	·0 − 3 = 7
					·3 − 4 = 9	·2 − 4 = 8	·1 − 4 = 7	·0 − 4 = 6
				·4 − 5 = 9	·3 − 5 = 8	·2 − 5 = 7	·1 − 5 = 6	·0 − 5 = 5
			·5 − 6 = 9	·4 − 6 = 8	·3 − 6 = 7	·2 − 6 = 6	·1 − 6 = 5	·0 − 6 = 4
		·6 − 7 = 9	·5 − 7 = 8	·4 − 7 = 7	·3 − 7 = 6	·2 − 7 = 5	·1 − 7 = 4	·0 − 7 = 3
	·7 − 8 = 9	·6 − 8 = 8	·5 − 8 = 7	·4 − 8 = 6	·3 − 8 = 5	·2 − 8 = 4	·1 − 8 = 3	·0 − 8 = 2
·8 − 9 = 9	·7 − 9 = 8	·6 − 9 = 7	·5 − 9 = 6	·4 − 9 = 5	·3 − 9 = 4	·2 − 9 = 3	·1 − 9 = 2	·0 − 9 = 1

In other words, when you're subtracting and you see 5 minus 8, you should automatically slash (the answer digit of the preceding column) and think 7 (15 minus 8).

And — when you see 4 minus 9, you should automatically slash and think 5 (14 minus 9).

With practice, the answers to all these subtraction possibilities will come to you automatically, just as quickly and naturally as the addition combinations you studied in the first chapter.

Study the two preceding tables of possibilities at length — until you have them down pat — and then see if you can promptly come up with the answers in this drill in subtraction possibilities (all you need do here is slash and then subtract the right-column digits).

1.
```
  4 ·2
-  2 7
  2̸ 5
  1 5
```

2.
```
  5 3
- 1 4
    4
```


3.
```
  7 4
- 3 8
    4
```

4.
```
  6 0
- 4 4
    2
```

5.
```
  3 0
-   6
    3
```


6.
```
  3 4
- 2 7
    1
```

7.
```
  8 3
- 1 5
    7
```

8.
```
  6 2
- 4 4
    2
```

9.	3 7 − 8 3	10.	4 6 − 2 9 2	11.	9 0 − 8 1 1
12.	3 8 − 1 9 2	13.	4 0 − 1 2 3	14.	5 5 − 2 6 3
15.	2 2 − 3 2	16.	4 2 − 2 4 2	17.	6 3 − 4 5 2
18.	6 3 − 3 4 3	19.	7 0 − 2 7 5	20.	4 2 − 1 8 3

WHAT HAVE YOU LEARNED SO FAR?

Now look back a moment to review what you've learned about subtraction . . . .

The one operation in subtraction which gets most people in trouble is "borrowing," because it asks you to do two things at once — to remember that you've borrowed from one number at the same time that you're trying to subtract from another.

Eliminate this need for double-memorizing — and you streamline subtraction to the point where you can do it nearly as fast as you can count.

Working from left to right, plus the One-Second Slash Method, does this for you. It eliminates the need to remember when you borrow.

Slashing a digit reduces its value by 1. It thus automatically raises the value of the next digit to its upper right by 10.

The One-Second Slash Method therefore frees your mind to concentrate on solving simple subtractions. Practice with this method will enable you to solve subtraction problems almost as quickly as you can read them.

IT WORKS ON EVERY PROBLEM

Although we haven't gone into it, it should be clear that these same general rules apply to all subtraction problems, no matter how many digits they may have. I think perhaps I should go into it just a bit. For example:

$$
\begin{array}{r}
3\ 1\ 4,4\ 7\ 1 \\
-\ 2\ 3\ 7,5\ 9\ 9 \\
\hline
\cancel{1}\ \cancel{8}\ \cancel{7},\cancel{9}\ \cancel{8}\ 2 \\
7\ 6,8\ 7\ 2
\end{array}
$$

Here's one more example:

$$
\begin{array}{r}
4\ 8\ 2\ 6 \\
-\ \ \ \ 9\ 4\ 3 \\
\hline
\cancel{4}\ \cancel{9}\ 8\ 3 \\
3\ 8\ 8\ 3
\end{array}
$$

Do you see how easy it is? The only time you might run into a problem is when you must slash a zero. The rule for this is as follows:

When you must borrow from a zero, slash it and
write a 9 beneath it, and then slash the DIGIT TO THE
LEFT of the zero.

```
    3 4 5              6 4 3 2
  - 2 4 6            - 2 2 3 6
  ̷1 ̷0 9             4 ̷2 ̷0 6
    9                    9
  _____              _____
    9 9              4 1 9 6
```

REVIEW QUIZ NO. 2

If you can't answer all of these questions, go back to
the beginning of this chapter and review the sections
that you haven't fully understood. Remember: the only
good mark is 100%.

1. What part of the conventional method of
   subtracting caused most errors?

2. How does the One-Second Slash, combined
   with working from left to right, eliminate
   the difficult part of borrowing?

3. What does a slash do to the numerical
   value of a number?

4. How does the slash affect the next digit
   to the upper right?

5. Can the slash be used in all subtraction
   problems?

6. Do I thoroughly understand the rules &
   principles in this chapter?

ANSWERS: ⯐1.⯐ Borrowing.

⯐2.⯐ It lets you record your borrowing on the paper immediately, and thus frees your mind to concentrate on nothing else but simple subtractions.

⯐3.⯐ It reduces it by 1.

⯐4.⯐ It raises its value by 10.

⯐5.⯐ Yes.

⯐6.⯐ Yes (I hope).

Did you correctly answer every one of the questions in Review Quiz No. 2? If not, you'd better reread this chapter, until you're sure that you understand this new, modern method of subtraction without borrowing.

If you did answer each of the questions correctly, you're ready for your final test in the practical application of what you've learned. Here it is:

YOUR FINAL EXAM IN SUBTRACTION WITHOUT BORROWING

1. How much will you owe on a $219 television set, after you've made a down payment of $21.90?

$$\$2\ 1\ 9\ .\ 0\ 0$$
$$-\ \ \ 2\ 1\ .\ 9\ 0$$

2. You're making the 705-mile drive from Saskatoon to Aberdeen, and by the time you've reached Jamestown you've traveled 599 miles. How far have you to go?

$$7\ 0\ 5$$
$$-\ 5\ 9\ 9$$

3. After your $143.22 take-home pay has been reduced by $18.75 through payroll savings plan, how much money will be left?

$$\begin{array}{r} \$1\,4\,3\,.\,2\,2 \\ -\ \ 1\,8\,.\,7\,5 \\ \hline \end{array}$$

4. If the Mets have already played 75 games of their 162-game season, how many more games remain in which to pull themselves out of the cellar?

$$\begin{array}{r} 1\,6\,2 \\ -\ \ \ 7\,5 \\ \hline \end{array}$$

5. If you have 4 yards of silk and the dress you want to make requires 2-1/2 yards, how much fabric can you expect to be left over after you've cut your pattern?

$$\begin{array}{r} 4\,.\,0 \\ -\ 2\,.\,5 \\ \hline \end{array}$$

6. A mile contains 1,760 yards; how much shorter than that distance is an 880-yard race?

$$\begin{array}{r} 1\,,\,7\,6\,0 \\ -\ \ \ 8\,8\,0 \\ \hline \end{array}$$

7. How many years will pass between 1965 and the end of the century?

$$\begin{array}{r} 2\,0\,0\,0 \\ -\ 1\,9\,6\,5 \\ \hline \end{array}$$

8. If someone gave you a million dollars and you had to pay $887,624 income tax, what would you have left?

$$\begin{array}{r} \$\ 1,000,000 \\ -\ \underline{887,624} \end{array}$$

9. The Sun is 93 <u>million</u> miles away from us, while the average distance between Earth and the Moon is a scant 238,857 miles. How much farther away from here, then, is the Sun?

$$\begin{array}{r} 93,000,000 \\ -\ \underline{238,857} \end{array}$$

10. If you pay $7.77 for an alarm clock out of a ten-dollar bill, how much change should you receive?

$$\begin{array}{r} \$\ 10.00 \\ -\ \underline{7.77} \end{array}$$

11. You've managed to save $19.75 toward the $39 rifle you want. How much more must you save?

$$\begin{array}{r} \$\ 39.00 \\ -\ \underline{19.75} \end{array}$$

12. The length of your lot of land is 122 feet, 6 inches, and the garage you plan to build at one end will measure 28 feet, 9 inches. How many feet of driveway will you need?

$$\begin{array}{r} 122.50 \quad \text{(122-1/2 feet)} \\ -\ \underline{28.75} \quad \text{(28-3/4 feet)} \end{array}$$

SPECIAL BONUS: SOME TIPS ON HOW TO
SUBTRACT EASILY AND MENTALLY

The most useful of all gadgets, when it comes to
streamlining subtraction with short cuts, is — zeros.

What I mean, of course, is that the happiest of all
possible digits to discover in a subtraction problem —
anywhere in a subtraction problem, and as frequently
as possible — are 0's. So the trick, in simplifying subtraction with short cuts, is to get those 0's in there.

There are two fundamental ways of doing this — one
crams them in all at once, while the other feeds them
one at a time.

ZEROING IN

Here's the first subtraction short cut: First calculate the difference between one of the problem's numbers
and a larger round number, ending with a zero or zeros,
then add that amount to both of the numbers in the problem.

For example:

$$
\begin{array}{ccc}
2\,6\,5\,0 & & 2\,6\,5\,9 \\
-\;\;\;4\,9\,1 & \text{becomes} & -\;\;\;5\,0\,0 \\
\hline
& & 2\,1\,5\,9
\end{array}
$$

Do you see how I did this? Since the bottom number
of that problem was only 9 less than 500, it was a simple matter to add 9 to both of the problem's numbers,
and subtract the easy-to-handle 500. That's zeroing
in, and that's all there is to it.

$$
\begin{array}{ccc}
3\,6\,1 & & 3\,6\,7 \\
-\;\;\;4\,4 & \text{(Add 6 to each to get a zero.)} & -\;\;\;5\,0
\end{array}
$$

The answer is easily and mentally arrived at . . . 317.

Obviously this device works best with problems in which one of the numbers is fairly close to a larger round number. Then it's quite simple to compute the quantity that must be added to both numbers in the problem.

Just remember that in subtraction, whatever is added to one number must also be added to the other. In that way, the difference remains unchanged.

Here are some subtraction problems for which the zeroing in device is applicable. Don't use paper to solve them. Make all those zeros mentally, and solve the problems in this

DRILL IN SUBTRACTING WITH
THE ZEROING-IN DEVICE

[1.]	723	[2.]	874	[3.]	4,723
	− 498		− 389		− 1,999

[4.]	8,431	[5.]	7,849	[6.]	3,849
	− 7,975		− 2,850		− 2,945

[7.]	8,743	[8.]	9,623	[9.]	5,723
	− 5,508		− 2,725		− 2,895

[10.]	6,435
	− 4,888

A ZERO AT A TIME

The last time I went through the supermarket, I got to the checkout counter and watched the register's numbers spin out a bill of $7.83. I handed the girl a ten-dollar bill, and she proceeded to give me what little change I had coming. She recited, $7.83 . . . $7.90 . . . $8.00 . . . and $2.00 makes $10.00.

And she was accomplishing it by <u>converting one digit at a time into a zero.</u> That's the principle — the "making change" aspect — of the <u>piece-work</u> device as it applies to subtraction.

But the top number of a subtraction problem — a real subtraction problem that you might have to solve any time at all — isn't very often as round as that ten-dollar bill! What on earth would you do with a problem like

$$8\ 4\ 7$$
$$-\ \underline{5\ 5\ 2}$$

Well, there are a few ways of handling it. You could take the 47 <u>away</u> from the 847 to get 800. Then take the same 47 away from 552 to get 505. 505 from 800 is easier to figure; and — arrive at 295. (Just think 500 from 800 is 300; but there's still a 5 to take away. So, 5 from 300 is 295.)

Or — after taking that 47 from 847, simply "make change" and subtract 552 from 800. (552 and 8 brings you to 560; another 40 — that's 48, so far — brings you to 600; 200 more, or 248 is the partial answer because it brings you to the 800.)

Now simply add the 47 you originally took away, to get <u>295.</u> Do it by "piece-work" as I've already taught you. 248 + <u>40</u> is 288; 288 + <u>7</u> is 295.

So, to conclude: If you're faced with the problem of 62 minus 47, add 3 to the 47 to make it 50; add 3 (to compensate) to 62 to make it 65. The problem now is, 65 minus 50 — the answer to which will immediately pop into your mind – 15.   62 minus 47 is 15. Of course, you could have subtracted 2 from 62 to make it 60; then subtract the same 2 from 47 to make it 45. 60 minus 45? Still 15!

Final example: 815 minus 369 looks formidable. But look: add 1 to each number, getting 816 minus 370. Now add 30 to each, getting 846 minus 400! The answer is obviously 446.   815 – 369 = 446.

FINAL DRILL IN MENTAL SUBTRACTION –
ZEROING-IN AND PIECE-WORK

1.	429	2.	876	3.	895	4.	975
	– 393		– 559		– 589		– 888

5.	4,327	6.	5,874
	– 2,885		– 3,995

7.	4,752	8.	23,456
	– 1,875		– 17,878

9.	45,678	10.	473,624
	– 26,789		– 88,888

Mathematical Miracle
Number Three—How To
Multiply Without Multiplying

Multiplication is actually extended addition. If you can eliminate its one stumbling block — carrying — you can multiply without actually multiplying! Working from left to right, you will simply record times-table products, automatically, and combine them without ever carrying a single figure. You'll solve multiplication problems involving any number of digits, as quickly as you can write down the answers.

Farmer (showing off his farm to a friend): "How many sheep would you say are in that flock? Take a rough guess."

Friend (after a short pause): "I'd say there are about 498 sheep."

Farmer: "Why, that's exactly right! How in the world did you guess?"

Friend: "It was simple, really. I just counted all the legs, and then divided by four."

I don't imagine you'll ever have to count the legs of sheep and then divide by four, but you have probably come across problems like this quite often:

A salesman sells 43 air conditioners to a contractor, earning a $36 commission on each machine . . .

$$
\begin{array}{r}
4\,3 \\
\times\,3\,6 \\
\hline
(?) \\
\hline
\$1,5\,4\,8
\end{array}
$$

A young man who needs five new tires for his jalopy learns that he can buy them for $21.77 apiece . . .

$$
\begin{array}{r}
\$\quad 2\,1\,.\,7\,7 \\
\times\,5 \\
\hline
(?) \\
\hline
\$1\,0\,8\,.\,8\,5
\end{array}
$$

Persian melons are 49¢ each; one hostess will need 16 of them to serve the guests at her dinner party . . .

$$
\begin{array}{r}
4\,9 \\
\times\,1\,6 \\
\hline
(?) \\
\hline
\$7\,.\,8\,4
\end{array}
$$

Multiplication is the one mathematical process which causes most people the most trouble. Although it comprises (according to statisticians who know about such things) only about one-fifth of all the figuring you do, it's usually the major part of problems for which you're in a hurry to get the answers — problems that are concerned with money, for instance.

When you're in a hurry, it's easy to make mistakes. And in multiplication, it's easy to make big mistakes . . . and harder to trace your errors, because more than one process has been involved.

MULTIPLICATION IS MORE COMPLEX
THAN ADDITION OR SUBTRACTION

I'm talking about the kind of multiplication problems
that come up every day. Problems like the ones at the
beginning of this chapter, involving the multiplication
of one two-digit number by another two-digit number,
or a four-digit number by a four-digit number, or even
a twelve-digit number by a seven-digit number.

Problems like these begin with simple "times-table"
multiplication. But then — if you're attempting to solve
them with conventional methods — they get complicated.

They get complicated by carrying (transferring sur-
plus bunches of units to the 10's column, and so on) —
and by long rows of addition — and by the necessity of
writing all those numbers in the correct columns. So
that the average multiplication problem ends up looking
like this:

$$
\begin{array}{r}
3\ 6\ 8 \\
\times\ 7\ 4\ 5 \\
\hline
1\ 8\ 4\ 0 \\
1\ 4\ 7\ 2 \\
2\ 5\ 7\ 6 \\
\hline
2\ 7\ 4\,,1\ 6\ 0
\end{array}
$$

See how many mistake-traps there are in this way
of doing the problem? Let's see if we can't eliminate
them.

In the last chapter we set out to overcome the diffi-
culties caused by the toughest part of subtraction —
borrowing; and we used modern mathematical techniques
to eliminate it entirely.

Now, in exactly the same way, I'm going to show you
a simple combination of techniques enabling you to do
multiplication problems more rapidly, more accurately,

more confidently than ever before . . . by eliminating
the most difficult part of multiplication — carrying.

THE OLD-FASHIONED WAY OF
SOLVING MULTIPLICATION PROBLEMS

The conventional way to multiply made it necessary
for you to carry one figure in your mind at exactly the
same time you were multiplying two other figures. Using a simple problem as an example, so that it's easier
to see each step, let's review how it was done:

$$\begin{array}{r} 4\,6 \\ \times\,9 \\ \hline 4\,1\,4 \end{array}$$

In this problem, first you multiplied 9 × 6 to get
54. (Note that you started backward, doing the problem
on the right end first, so that you'd have someplace to
"carry" the left-hand digit of your product.)

That was your first step. Then you wrote down the
right-hand digit of that 54 — 4 — and "carried" the
left-hand digit — 5 — in your mind to the next task of
multiplication — 9 × 4.

Now you multiplied 9 × 4 to get 36, and added the
5 you were carrying to get 41. And this is your answer.

See how difficult it is! In a problem involving two
numbers of, say, four digits each, by the time you have
performed each multiplication, you'd probably have
forgotten which numbers you are "carrying" where!

And if, by some chance, you remembered which numbers you were carrying, you would have made errors
in multiplication because you were simultaneously con-
centrating on which number to carry.

And if you could remember which numbers you were
carrying, and still be able to perform your multiplica-

tions at exactly the same time without making errors, then you still would have been slowed down considerably in your calculating, at the very least.

There had to be a way of improving and simplifying this method of multiplication. There had to be a way to eliminate the confusing, time-wasting step of thinking about two things at one time.

In order to discover a better way of multiplying, mathematicians had to take a closer look at the process of multiplication itself. They had to take it apart and put it back together, in a way that would make the most difficult multiplication problem as simple to solve as the easiest calculation.

And that's just what they did, and what I'm going to show you.

WHAT IS MULTIPLICATION?

What does a multiplication problem mean, anyway? It means this: 46 × 9 is actually just a short way of adding nine 46's (46 + 46 + 46 + 46 + 46 + 46 + 46 + 46 + 46). And the technique that evolved for computing the answer to such an "extended addition" problem (for that's all it really is), was utilization of multiplication tables — the "times-tables" you learned at school.

For example, instead of adding nine 6's, you simply drew on your memory of these times-tables and decided, more or less by rote, that nine 6's are 54. You had memorized these times-tables. You knew them by heart and you automatically wrote down the answer.

NOW LET'S START MAKING MULTIPLICATION EASY

Simplifying the problem still further — since 46 is actually a short way of writing 40 + 6 — then 46 × 9 is actually a short way of writing (40 × 9) + (6 × 9). And it can be worked out this way:

```
      4 6
    × 9
    3 6 0  (40 ×  9)
  +   5 4  ( 6 ×  9)
    4 1 4
```

And right there is the clue to one of the most important secrets of streamlining the entire process of multiplication:

<u>Break each problem down into a series of times-table calculations, and add their answers</u>!

```
      3 4
    × 8
    2 4 0  (8 × 30)
  +   3 2  (8 ×  4)
    2 7 2
```

```
      4 6
    × 3 7
    1 2 0 0  (30 × 40)
  +   1 8 0  (30 ×  6)
  +   2 8 0  ( 7 × 40)
  +     4 2  ( 7 ×  6)
    1 7 0 2
```

$$
\begin{array}{r}
4\ 8\ 4 \\
\times\ 6\text{-}1/2 \\
\hline
\end{array}
$$

	2 4 0 0	(6 × 400)
+	4 8 0	(6 × 80)
+	2 4	(6 × 4)
+	2 0 0	(1/2 × 400)
+	4 0	(1/2 × 80)
+	2	(1/2 × 4)
	3 1 4 6	

By doing multiplication this way, the only actual multiplying you'll ever have to do will involve single digits. And that means that you can do the multiplication part of the most complicated problems using nothing more than grade-school times-tables!

Can you see the beauty of this idea? Can you see how easy every multiplication problem becomes when you think of it as really nothing more than a group of simple times-table problems?

All you need to know to solve any multiplication problem, then, would be:

1. Your grade-school times-table; and

2. A foolproof method of writing these times-tables products in the proper places.

This way, you'll convert each multiplication problem into a much easier problem in addition. And the way to do that — the way to multiply without multiplying — is so simple that you'll wonder why it wasn't taught to you in school.

ALWAYS WORK FROM LEFT TO RIGHT

You've certainly become convinced, by now, that the best direction in working with numbers is the direction in which you read them — <u>forward</u>, from left to right.

That's the logical way, because you solve the <u>im-
portant</u> part of any problem, at the very beginning. In
multiplication, for example, it's more important to
know that 23 × 3 are 60-something, than that the correct answer is something-9.

Now, in multiplying without multiplying, the secret
to working <u>correctly</u> from left to right lies in <u>knowing
where to start:</u> knowing automatically <u>just where</u> to record each times-table product. Once you know this
simple secret, you don't even have to bother writing in
all the zeros, as we did in our sample problems above.

And the secret is as simple as this. Let's look at
a sample problem:

$$
\begin{array}{r}
4\ 6 \\
\times\ 9 \\
\hline
\end{array}
$$

    3 6   (9 × 4) (Step 1)
    5 4   (9 × 6) (Step 2)

In this problem of 46 × 9, the first thing you do is
multiply 9 × 4. <u>But that 4 is actually 40, so what you</u>
<u>are</u> actually multiplying is 9 × 40.

Now 9 × 40 involves <u>three</u> digits. So the 36 (which
is actually 360) is recorded in a position beginning
<u>three</u> columns from the end. (Not the beginning, but the
<u>end</u> — the <u>right</u> end).

And, by the same reasoning, the second times-table
problem, which is 9 × 6, involves just <u>two</u> digits. And
so its answer (54) is recorded <u>two</u> columns in from the
end.

All you're really doing is <u>counting</u> the digits you're
multiplying (<u>plus those to the right of them</u>). By simply
counting these digits, you'll know exactly how many
spaces from the end to start writing your answer.

After you've performed both of the times-table calculations in this problem, and recorded their products, you've only to add the columns to get the answer. This is what they look like, now:

3 6

 5 4

In a simple situation like this, all you have to do is follow the procedure which you learned in Chapter One for calculating the final sum in long addition problems. Work from left to right, and before writing in the total of any column, sneak a peek at its right-hand neighboring digits; if its neighbors equal or exceed 10, raise its value by 1. Remember? So here's your answer;

3 6   3 6

 5 4 — or, use the underline   5 4

4 1 4   3 1 4 = 4 1 4

Now, do you understand the method of determining where to record the times-table products in a multiplication problem? To make absolutely certain, here's another example:

3 4

× 6 7

The first calculation in this problem is 6 × 3. But that 3, of course, is actually 30, and that 6 is actually 60. So what you are actually multiplying is 30 × 60.

Now, 60 × 30 involves four digits, which means that you will record the times-table product of 6 × 3 (18) four columns to the left of the end of the whole problem, like this:

3 4

× 6 7

1 8

Actually, what you've written here is 1800. But, since we don't want to write in the zeros, you simply leave them out. The next calculation is 6 × 4 (which actually signifies 60 × 4). 60 × 4 involves three digits. Therefore you start this times-table product three columns to the left.

But this time, you write the 4 of your product of 24 at the HIGHEST possible point in its column! (Even if that means two or three horizontal columns up.)

```
           3 4                        3 4
          × 6 7                      × 6 7
Like this: 1 8 4    Not like this:   1 8
           2                         2 4
```

There's a very good reason for writing each digit as high as you can in its column: you do it to save space.

In a very long problem, one involving numbers that contain several digits, simply writing down all of the times-table products, one under the other, would take up much more space than is really necessary.

Instead, by writing each digit of each times-table product at the highest available space in its column, you can eliminate as much as half of your writing space.

We'll see how this works as we go on with our sample problem.

Continue, then, with the next step in the example — 7 × 3, which actually signifies 7 × 30. Since there are three digits in 7 × 30, start writing the answer (21) three columns from the end:

```
                    3 4                           3 4
                  × 6 7                         × 6 7
 Like this:       1 8 4     Not like this:      1 8 4
                    2 1                           2
                    2                             2 1
```

Notice — the 2 of the 21, going three columns from the end, goes under the 2 (of 24). The 1 of the 21 goes into the next highest available space — directly under the 4 (of 24).

The next simple times-table step is 7 × 4. Since there are only two digits involved, the answer (28) is started two columns from the right end.

```
                    3 4                           3 4
                  × 6 7                         × 6 7
 Like this:       1 8 4 8   Not like this:      1 8 4
                    2 1                           2 1
                    2 2                           2 2 8
```

Now add the three answer rows using the sneak-a-peak, or underline, technique:

```
 1 8 4 8              1 8 4 8
   2 1     or           2 1
   2 2                   2 2
 2 2 7 8              1 2 7 8  =  2 2 7 8
```

And there you have it. The perfect answer, done in half the time and with half the trouble.

Please keep in mind that with all these new methods, since they are new to you, it will take some time and practice before they become second nature. So, even though they may seem clumsy at first, try them. Do the drills. And pretty soon you'll see their value.

I think it's time now for you to try your hand at a few more multiplication problems. Remember to work from left to right and multiply only two digits at a time, thereby eliminating the part of multiplication that used to mean trouble: carrying.

Remember: Count digits to determine where to record each times-table product.

FIRST DRILL IN EASY MULTIPLICATION

1.	4 9	2.	5 3	3.	6 9
	× 8		× 7		× 8

4.	8 8	5.	7 6	6.	6 3
	× 8		× 7		× 4 8

7.	7 9	8.	5 8	9.	9 9
	× 2 4		× 3 7		× 4 4

10.	6 2
	× 5 8

THIRTEEN BUG-A-BOOS

Now let's take a quick look at the thirteen times-table possibilities whose products (answers) are <u>single</u> digits. They can mean trouble unless you follow this simple rule:

Consider every single-digit product as a two-digit number whose first digit is a zero.

For example, as a times-table product, 6 is really 06; 9 is 09; 4 is 04.

Here's why:

	2 7		2 7
Not this way:	× 3	But this way:	× 3
	6		0 6 1
	2 1		2
			8 1

Let me show you the wrong and right ways to solve this problem.

If you were to attempt to solve it without this new rule, as in the example on the left, here's what you'd probably do. You'd realize immediately that 3 × 2 actually signifies 3 × 20. (Remember: simply count the digits you're multiplying and those to the right.) Since there are three digits in 3 × 20, you'd start to write your answer three columns to the left. This would lead you to write 6(00), and your final answer would be off by 540, since 3 × 20 = 60, not 600.

But by realizing that 3 × 2(0) is only a single-digit product and therefore equals 06(0), instead of 60(0), as in the example on the right, the correct answer — 81 — is inescapable. (Remember: any single-digit product is thought of with a zero (0) in front of it.)

One more example: To multiply 38 by 2 (you understand, of course, that in many of my examples, as in this, I'm not suggesting that these simple problems should be done on paper. I use them only to explain and demonstrate certain points you'll have to know when faced with complicated problems) you'd do this:

```
      3 8                        3 8
      × 2      Not this:         × 2
     0 6 6                       6
       1                         1 6
      ───                       ─────
      7 6
```

After you become more accustomed to this technique, you'll know when you can ignore zeros altogether. As in the above example, if you know the rule, you'll place the first 6 in the correct place and you needn't write the 0 at all.

Here are the thirteen bug-a-boos, and their debugged products:

1 × 1 = 01

1 × 2 = 02   2 × 2 = 04

1 × 3 = 03   2 × 3 = 06   3 × 3 = 09

1 × 4 = 04   2 × 4 = 08

1 × 5 = 05

1 × 6 = 06

1 × 7 = 07

1 × 8 = 08

1 × 9 = 09

And here, while I'm in the mood, are the other thirty-two possible times-table calculations you'll be called upon to solve from time to time:

$9 \times 9 = 81$

$8 \times 8 = 64$ $8 \times 9 = 72$

$7 \times 7 = 49$ $7 \times 8 = 56$ $7 \times 9 = 63$

$6 \times 6 = 36$ $6 \times 7 = 42$ $6 \times 8 = 48$ $6 \times 9 = 54$

$5 \times 5 = 25$ $5 \times 6 = 30$ $5 \times 7 = 35$ $5 \times 8 = 40$ $5 \times 9 = 45$

$4 \times 4 = 16$ $4 \times 5 = 20$ $4 \times 6 = 24$ $4 \times 7 = 28$ $4 \times 8 = 32$ $4 \times 9 = 36$

$3 \times 4 = 12$ $3 \times 5 = 15$ $3 \times 6 = 18$ $3 \times 7 = 21$ $3 \times 8 = 24$ $3 \times 9 = 27$

$2 \times 5 = 10$ $2 \times 6 = 12$ $2 \times 7 = 14$ $2 \times 8 = 16$ $2 \times 9 = 18$

The modern streamlining methods discussed in this chapter depend, just as did the old-fashioned method of multiplying, on the times-tables.

Therefore, <u>master</u> those times-tables. Drill yourself on them until you can rattle off the answers to any multiplication problem with the speed that you already have in addition.

And multiplication without multiplying, no matter how seemingly complex the problem, will be no more than a matter of writing down numbers as you read the problems and solve them automatically.

I think it's time, now, for you to try your hand at a few more multiplication problems, utilizing the time-saving techniques and devices you've learned in this chapter.

Let's review these new mathematical techniques briefly:

1. <u>Work from left to right</u>. It's the logical, sensible, most meaningful way to do multiplication problems . . . and it makes your method of recording times-tables products foolproof.

2. To determine the correct place in which to write each individual times-table product, <u>count the number of digits involved in each calculation</u>. In the problem of 46 × 37, for example, the first calculation of 3 × 4 actually signifies 30 × 40. . . which means four digits. So you start your answer four digits, or spaces, from the right.

To repeat, the simplest way to determine the amount of digits in any particular calculation, is to <u>count to the right from each of the digits you're using in the individual calculation</u>.

3. And don't forget the thirteen bug-a-boos; times-table calculations whose products are less than 10: <u>Consider every single-digit product as a two-digit number whose first digit is a zero</u>.

Now apply these time-saving devices by going to work on this

DRILL IN MULTIPLYING WITHOUT MULTIPLYING

1.
```
    2 6
  × 9
  1 8 4
    5
  2 3 4
```

2.
```
    3 8
  × 8
```

3.
```
    4 7
  × 2 6
```

4.
```
  6 , 7 8 9
      × 9
```

5.
```
    4 9
  × 3
```

6.
```
    6 4
  × 3 8
```

7.
```
  4 8 , 8 9 7
      × 1 2
```

8.
```
    6 4
  × 2 1
```

9.
```
    2 8
  × 8 2
```

10.
```
    6 9
  × 3 7
```

11.
```
    8 3
  × 7 7
```

12.
```
  3 4 6
  × 3 8
```

Did that last problem throw you? As the number of digits increases, and the columns of times-table products get longer, it becomes more and more difficult to peek at the neighboring column and quickly determine whether or not it equals 10 or more. So, let's stress the other weapon in the battle against misbehaving numbers — the symbol in our growing arsenal of mathematical shorthand, which I've sort of neglected up to now — the underline.

THE UNDERLINE

So far we know that <u>dot</u> = 10 . . . <u>Slash</u> = minus 1 . . . and <u>Underline</u> = plus 1. Whenever you underline a number, you increase its value by 1. <u>7</u> = 8; <u>4</u> = 5; <u>9</u> = 10.

You already know that, and it eliminates entirely a source of confusion in adding times-table products. It can increase your speed by 20% in solving multiplication problems.

And remember, you can even put <u>two</u> (or more) underlines beneath a number, to increase its value by <u>two</u>, (or more). <u>3</u> = 4, 3̳ = 5; 3̳ = 6.

Just to make sure that you're completely comfortable with this concept, work out the correct answers for this.

DRILL IN UNDERLINED DIGITS

<u>4</u> =   7̳ =   <u>3</u> =   <u>9</u> =   1̳ =

5̳ =   4̳ =   6̳ =   2̳ =   <u>8</u> =

<u>8</u> =   4̳ =   <u>3</u> =   6̳ =   5̳ =

7̳ =   1̳ =   9̳ =   2̳ =   <u>6</u> =

HOW THIS UNDERLINE SIMPLIFIES MULTIPLICATION

As you learned in the chapter on addition, when you add columns of figures, <u>if the total of a column exceeds or equals 10, write only the right-hand digit beneath it and underline the previous answer-digit once for every 10 units</u>. Like this:

```
   3 7
 + 4 8
   7 5   —   8 5
```

In a multiple-digit multiplication problem, the <u>underline</u> would be used this way:

```
        6 8 9
      × 7 6
    4 2 6 3 4
      5 6 8
      3 6 5
        4
    4
```

You see, of course, that your first calculation, 7 × 6, involves <u>five</u> digits (count to the right). So the first product, or answer (42), is started <u>five</u> spaces from the end.

In this sample problem, all the times-table products and the answer-digit of the first column are already written in, so that we can get right down to seeing the <u>underline</u> at work.

The second column (2 + 5 + 3) equals 10; write the zero beneath the column, and <u>underline</u> the previous answer-digit — the 4.

```
        6 8 9
        × 7 6
   ───────────
   4 2 6 3 4
     5 6 8
     3 6 5
       4
   ───────────
   4 0
   ─
```

At this point you can already see that the answer to this problem will be somewhere near 50,000. You've quickly arrived at an accurate estimate because you're working from left to right.

Add the third column, now: 6 + 6 + 6 + 4 = 22. Write the right-hand digit (2) beneath the column, and underline the previous answer-digit twice — to account for the left-hand digit of the column sum (22).

```
        6 8 9
        × 7 6
   ───────────
   4 2 6 3 4
     5 6 8
     3 6 5
       4
   ───────────
   4 0 2
   ─ ─
```

Proceed to the next column: 3 + 8 + 5 = 16; write the 6 beneath the column, and underline the answer-digit of the previous column once.

```
          6  8  9
        × 7  6
    _____
    4  2  6  3  4
       5  6  8
       3  6  5
       4
    _____
    4  0  2  6
```

The last column, of course, adds to 4, with no underlining required. So the answer — although it has yet to
be translated into a more familiar form — is 4 0, 2 6 4.
And, since each underlining of a digit increases its
value by 1, the correct answer to the problem is 52,364.

The 4 and the 2 — the digits which had a single underline beneath each of them — were increased to 5 and
3, respectively. The 0 , with two underlines beneath it,
was raised to 2. Therefore 4 0 , 2 6 4 equals 52,364.

The use of the underline in your bag of tricks makes
multiplication as easy as addition or subtraction. And
with the combination of devices you've learned in this
chapter, you can multiply without multiplying, in complete confidence.

ONE LAST WORD

Before your Review Quiz Number Three and your
Final Exam in Multiplication Without Multiplying, once
again let's go over the information you've learned.

Multiplication is more complex than addition or subtraction, because it involves several steps — including,
in the old-fashioned method of multiplying, carrying.

Carrying was the stumbling block in conventional
multiplication, because it required that you keep mental
track of several digits at the same time that you were
performing calculations of times-table products. There-

fore, if you could eliminate carrying, you'd be "<u>multi-plying without multiplying!</u>"

Multiplication is actually a problem in extended addition. Therefore, the way to eliminate carrying is as simple as this:

1. Work from left to right.

2. Multiply only two digits at a time. And write down their product immediately.

3. Determine the correct position of this product by counting the number of digits involved in the individual calculation, and starting to write the product the same number of columns from the end. (60 × 40 has <u>four</u> digits. Therefore you start to write its answer four columns in from the end of the problem.)

4. Consider all one-digit products to be two-digit numbers whose first digit is a zero. (4 × 2 = 08)

5. Always write each digit of each product at the highest available point in its column. This can save as much as 50% of the space required for doing the problem.

6. If the problem is a long one, use the <u>underline</u> method for totaling the columns. Write in the digits as you go along, and raise their value whenever necessary by underlining them — one underline for each unit to be raised. ($\underline{3}$ = 4; $\underline{\underline{3}}$ = 5.)

REVIEW QUIZ NO. 3

If you can't answer <u>all</u> of these questions, go back to the beginning of this chapter and review the sections that you haven't fully understood. Remember: the only acceptable mark is 100%.

> **1.** a. What part of the conventional method of multiplication causes confusion and errors?
>
> b. Why?

2. How is this cured by working from left to
right and correct positioning of times-
table products?

3. What is the correct way of positioning
times-table products?

4. Why is it necessary to precede all single-
digit products with a zero?

5. What is the underline method of increasing
digits?

6. Do you thoroughly understand the techniques taught in this chapter?

ANSWERS:

1. a. Carrying.

b. Because it makes it necessary to remember one set of numbers at the
same exact time you're trying to multiply another set of numbers.

2. By enabling you to simply multiply two
digits — write down the answer — and go
on to the next multiplication, without any
carrying or confusion!

3. Step one: count the number of digits in the
two figures being multiplied (including all
zeros). (Or simply count from the digits
to the right.) Step two: start to write the
answer the same number of columns in
from the end of the problem. And Step
three: place the second digit in the next
highest available space.

4. Because otherwise you would get too high
an answer. This zero technique gives you
the right positioning, automatically.

⟦5.⟧   It is used when you <u>add</u> the columns at the bottom of your answer. You add from left to right, of course. And when one column totals more than 10, you simply underline the answer-digit <u>to the left</u> to raise its value accordingly.

⟦6.⟧   Yes.

Remember: if you weren't able to answer these questions completely and correctly, you must reread this chapter until you have a thorough command of the techniques involved in multiplying-without-multiplying. Then, when you've mastered the subject, test yourself with this

FINAL EXAM IN MULTIPLYING WITHOUT MULTIPLYING

1. Your living room is 245 square feet in area, and the one-foot-square tiles you want to install will cost 23¢ each. How much will you pay for enough tiles to cover the floor?

$$
\begin{array}{r}
2\ 4\ 5 \\
\times\ .2\ 3 \\
\hline
\end{array}
$$

2. Your boss pays you $3.56 per hour overtime, and last month you stayed late a total of 47 hours. How much extra did you earn?

$$
\begin{array}{r}
3\ .\ 5\ 6 \\
\times\ 4\ 7 \\
\hline
\end{array}
$$

3. If 59 planks, each 3/4 inch thick, were stacked, how high would the stack be?

```
  5 9
× .7 5  (3/4)
```

4. Your fire insurance cost 53 cents per $100. How much does it cost you to insure your home for $17,500?

```
1 7 , 5 0 0
    × .5 3
```

5. What would 43 drums of oil weigh altogether, if each drum weighed 260 pounds?

```
  2 6 0
× 4 3
```

6. If the drive to your summer cabin is 357 miles each way, how many miles would you pile up each year in 12 round trips?

```
  3 5 7
× 2 4
```

7. The profit on the retail sale of a book is 94¢. If 3,678 books are sold, what is the total profit?

```
3 , 6 7 8
    × .9 4
```

8. The uniform for each member of the marching band requires 1-1/4 yards of green silk. How much green silk will be needed if uniforms are to be made for 62 members?

```
1 . 2 5   (1-1/4)
× 6 2
```

9. If your body requires 2,848 calories every day, how many will it need in 1980 (leap year)?

```
2 , 8 4 8
× 3 6 6
```

10. A manufacturer receives an order for 8,659 bags of sand, each bag to weigh 1 <u>long</u> ton (2,240 pounds). How many pounds of sand <u>is</u> all that?

```
8 , 6 5 9
× 2 , 2 4 0
```

Did some of the problems containing zeros throw you? They shouldn't have. Just do what comes naturally. In the problem

```
      2 6 0
      × 4 3
  0 8 4 8 0
    2 6
    0 1
  0 0 1 8 0
  1 1 1 8 0
```

When you come to 4 × 0, the answer is 0, so you just ignore it. Putting it down wouldn't change your answer and it would take up extra space. For the last calculation, 3 × 0, you could have omitted the answer (0), but it requires no extra space to fill in that last available space at the right of the first horizontal row.

And the problem of 17,500 × 53¢ should have looked like this:

```
      1 7 5 0 0
          × 5 3
  0 5 5 5 5 0 0
    3 2 1
    0 3 1
    2
  8 2 7 5. 0 0      — $9,275.00
```

Have you got all that? Are you sure? If not, you'd better reread this chapter. Review each drill; think as you read and work!

CHAPTER FIVE

How To Solve
"Impossible" Multiplication
Problems—In Your Head

A collection of short-cut devices that will save you time, money, and headaches . . . enable you to solve many complex problems in your head . . . show you how to do difficult problems with just a few quick scribbles . . . help you to make accurate mental estimates quickly and confidently, in the office and at meetings and conferences.

"Simplify, simplify." — Henry David Thoreau

Pause a moment to realize one extra advantage of the short cuts you've just learned.

Anyone can make a <u>game</u> out of multiplication, simply by utilizing the methods and techniques of Modern Mathematics which I described in the last few pages.

When you attack them from left to right, even the most complex multiplication problems become nothing more than a group of times-table calculations — asking only that they be properly recorded and <u>added</u>.

Like everything else in Modern Mathematics, you find the correct answer to your multiplication problems by <u>simplifying the task at hand</u> — by <u>exchanging a difficult procedure for a far simpler procedure</u>.

Now — in exactly the same way, a large number of multiplication problems <u>can be reduced even further.</u>

For example, quite often it just isn't <u>convenient</u> for you to sit down with a pad and pencil to solve problems requiring an immediate answer. So there are many specialized techniques and devices you can use to shorten the work of solving certain problems considerably. So much so that you can do them with little or no paperwork . . . many of them <u>in your head, in seconds.</u>

LET'S TAKE A FEW EVERYDAY EXAMPLES

Do you think you could solve problems like this <u>almost instantly</u> — and/or — <u>without paper and pencil:</u>

1 0 3	6 2 4 2	7 1 2	5 1 3
× 7 2	× 7 2 0	× 7 7	× 5 1

7 6	2 9	3 5	1 2 4 8
× 1 8	× 1 6	× 9 9	× 1 2 5

And many, many more?

Well, read on and you'll learn how easy it is to come up with the answers to problems like this — fast!

What do you do when you come across a problem like this?

<u>What is the cost of 35 fountain pens @ 99¢ each?</u>

Using the modern methods of multiplication which you learned in Chapter Four, the solution would be:

```
    $ .9 9
     × 3 5
  2 7 7 5
    2 5
    4 4
  2 3 6 5  —  $ 3 4 . 6 5
```

That's a good bit faster than the old-fashioned way
of multiplying backward, with all its carrying and confusion. But how about this solution of the same problem:

```
  3 5 0 0
   – 3 5
  3 5 7 5  —  $ 3 4 . 6 5
```

Do you see what I did? I just used the easiest way of
multiplying a number by 99. First, I multiplied that
number (35) by 100 (as you remember from school, to
multiply any number by 100, simply tack on two zeros).
And then I simply subtracted that same number (35)
from the total (3500) once.

In most cases, you can perform these simple processes in your head. But even if you couldn't, you'd
be far ahead of the game by using this shortcut. Even
if you can't multiply 576,872,649 by 99 mentally, you
can certainly work it out faster with this device than
you could any other way: (Again, multiply it by 100 and
then subtract the number itself, once, like this:)

```
    5 7 6 8 7 2 6 4 9 0 0
  –     5 7 6 8 7 2 6 4 9
    5 7 1 1 7 4 9 2 3 5 1  —  57,110,392,251
```

There are countless short-cut devices like this that
can save hours of unnecessary calculating. In fact, for

practically every single multiplication problem, there is at least one way of cutting time, in addition to the time saved by recording and adding times-table products.

These simple techniques range from a device — almost universally known — for multiplying by 10 (adding one zero) . . . to another device — which hardly anyone at all knows — for determining whether a large number is divisible by 7.

In this chapter I'll show you several multiplication short cuts, which you can use to simplify the paperwork you must perform, or to eliminate that paperwork.

Using these short cuts, you'll amaze your friends as you come up with the answers to "impossible" problems, in seconds! You'll impress those with whom you work with your ability to offer the right figures repeatedly at conferences. You'll feel the satisfaction of knowing the right answers to complicated problems involving household projects, card games, and money matters — in most cases, without even reaching for a piece of paper.

I promise you that with very little effort you'll get "miraculous" results, using these modern short cut techniques. They're all designed to simplify a problem — to make it genuinely easy for you to calculate, step-by-step, the correct answer.

And, after you learn these techniques, your only problem will be to decide which time-slasher to use — to get the job done in a flash.

THE FIRST SHORT-CUT DEVICE —
"MENTAL BREAKDOWN"

Mental Breakdown can slash as much as 90% from the time it takes to multiply certain numbers. I said certain numbers — because you can't use mental breakdown to solve every multiplication problem. That's why there are many other streamlining devices in miracle mathematics.

But you'll be able to apply <u>mental breakdown</u> to enough problems, so that it will be well worth your while to learn this simple short cut. When you multiply by certain numbers like 44, 99, 63, 125, 15, 18, 19, 21, 402, 505, 550, 72, 270, and many others, whose properties you'll understand shortly, <u>mental breakdown</u> can do practically <u>all</u> the work for you. It can actually show you how to solve some of these problems entirely in your head.

For example, that device for multiplying by 99 — the trick of multiplying the number by 100 and then subtracting it from the product — that's an example of the <u>mental breakdown</u> method of simplifying multiplication.

It's much <u>easier</u> to work with 100 <u>and</u> 1 than to attempt multiplication by 99. And that's exactly what <u>mental breakdown is</u>: <u>Breaking down a hard-to-handle number into two easier-to-handle numbers</u>.

The object of the <u>mental breakdown</u> device is to <u>simplify your work by exchanging a difficult process for an easy one — even two easy ones, if they're easy enough.</u>

Multiplying a number by 10, or by 100, or by 1,000, is about as simple as any calculation can be . . . right? To multiply by 10, you simply add a zero. To multiply by 100, add two zeros; by 1,000, add <u>three</u> zeros. It's simplicity itself.

If multiplying by 10 is so easy, and multiplying by 1 isn't multiplying at all, then naturally you'd use <u>mental breakdown</u> every time you must solve a problem involving multiplication by 11 (10 + 1), 99 (100 – 1), 101 (100 + 1), 900 (1,000 – 100), 990 (1,000 – 10), 999 (1,000 – 1) and so on.

Let's run through one or two examples now and prove how incredibly easy it is.

First, suppose you want to know the cost of a gross of rain hats that are 99¢ each. All you do is this:

$$
\begin{array}{r}
1\,4\,4 \\
\times\ .9\,9 \\
\end{array}
\ =\
\begin{array}{r}
\$\,1\,4\,4\,.\,0\,0 \qquad (144 \times 100) \\
\$\,-\ \ 1\,.\,4\,4 \qquad (144 \times 1) \\
\hline
\$\,1\,4\,\cancel{3}\ \ \cancel{0}\,6\ =\ \$\,1\,4\,2\,.\,5\,6
\end{array}
$$

See how simple it is!

Now, let's try a problem with 101 — in which you
add the number being multiplied to the product of itself
and 100. What is the cost of 101 pounds of cloth at
$7.89 per pound?

$$
\begin{array}{r}
\$\,7\,.\,8\,9 \\
\times\ \ 1\,0\,1 \\
\end{array}
\ =\
\begin{array}{r}
\$\,7\,8\,9\,.\,0\,0 \qquad (789 \times 100) \\
+\ \ \ \ 7\ \ \ 8\,9 \qquad (789 \times 1) \\
\hline
\$\,7\,8\,6\ \ \ 8\,9\ =\ \$\,7\,9\,6\,.\,8\,9
\end{array}
$$

Incidently, did you notice how we used both the slash
and the underline to help reach these answers even more
quickly? The slash and the underline simplify the processes of subtraction and addition, as you learned in the
early chapters.

And the device of mental breakdown simplifies many
multiplication problems by converting them to easier-
to-do processes of addition and subtraction.

I've shown you what to do when multiplying any number by 99 or 101. You probably already realize that, to
multiply a number by 999, you'd simply add three zeros
to the number and then subtract the number once. (999 ×
87 can be considered 87000 minus 87.)

To multiply any number by 1,001, simply tack on
three zeros and add the number once. To multiply any
number by 1,010, tack on three zeros, then add ten times
the number. (1,010 × 712 can be considered 712,000
plus 7120.)

And, of course, to multiply any number by 990, simply tack on the three zeros and then subtract ten times
the number. (990 × 831 can be considered 831,000
minus 8310.)

Now . . . using the device of <u>mental breakdown</u> see how quickly you can solve the problems in this

DRILL NO. 1 IN MENTAL BREAKDOWN

[1.]	365 × 99	[2.]	8765 ×101	[3.]	14,675,982 × 99

[4.]	1010 × 638	[5.]	564 ×990	[6.]	4563 ×999

[7.]	1,001 ×8,549	[8.]	642,578 ×1,010	[9.]	$3366 ×101

[10.]	2,322 ×299

Now how <u>about</u> that last problem, 2,322 × 299? Did you find the best way, the easiest way to solve it?

Did you see that you could get the answer by multiplying 2,322 by <u>300</u> (multiply by 3, then add two zeros) — to get 696,600 — and then subtracting 2,322 from that product?

If you did the problem correctly, you should have been able to determine that the answer was 694,278, <u>without</u> touching a pencil to paper.

You just multiplied a four-digit number by a three-digit number, <u>in your head</u>. Did you ever think you'd be able to accomplish that "impossible" feat?

As you learn other uses of the <u>mental breakdown</u>

techniques — and as you learn other short-cut devices — you'll begin to see how each has a place in your arsenal of modern mathematical miracles. You need only select the best weapon or weapons to level against any multiplication problem, and fire away.

OTHER BENEFITS OF THE MENTAL BREAKDOWN TECHNIQUE

As I've already stated, the purpose of the mental breakdown technique is to simplify your work by exchanging a difficult process for a simpler one — to break down a hard-to-work-with number into two easy-to-work-with numbers.

But, if the only hard-to-work-with numbers to which the mental breakdown technique could be applied were 99's and 101's, its use would be quite limited. But fortunately there are an infinite number of ways to use mental breakdown so that it applies to an unlimited number of numbers.

For instance, suppose you were faced with the problem of multiplying 324 by 98. Why not multiply 324 by 100 — to get 32400 — and then subtract 2 × 324 (because 98 is 2 less than 100), or 648. This would give you the correct answer — 31,752 — in seconds.

To make it easier to write, I'll use a simple equation or formula to describe some of these processes. The letter N will mean "number," and when used like this: 100N; it will mean 100 times the number. So the formula for the mental breakdown for 324 × 98 would be 100N − 2N: 100 times the number minus two times the number.

True, there are two steps (multiplying by 100 is so simple that I don't even count it as a step) to perform: (1) doubling the number, and (2) subtracting. But these can be done mentally. And this makes 324 × 98 a problem which can be solved in your head, simply by utilizing the technique of mental breakdown.

Similarly, any number which can be "rounded off" to an easier-to-work-with number, is food for the mental breakdown technique. How about 97 (100N – 3N) . . . 9,800 (10,000N – 200N) . . . 1,020 (1,000N + 20N) . . . 52 (50N + 2N) . . . 27 (30N – 3N) . . . 48 (50N – 2N) . . . and so on, to infinity.

They're as easy to do as this:

$$
\begin{array}{r}
8\,3\,3 \\
\times\,9\,9\,7 \\
\end{array}
\quad \text{becomes} \quad
\begin{array}{r}
8\,3\,3\,0\,0\,0 \quad (1{,}000 \times 833) \\
-\ 2\,4\,9\,9 \quad (3 \times 833) \\
\hline
8\,3\,\cancel{1}\,\cancel{0}\,\cancel{1}\,1\ -\ 830{,}501
\end{array}
$$

$$
\begin{array}{r}
1\,0\,3 \\
\times\ \ 7\,2 \\
\end{array}
\text{ becomes }
\begin{array}{r}
7\,2 \\
\times\,1\,0\,3 \\
\end{array}
\text{ which becomes }
\begin{array}{r}
7\,2\,0\,0 \quad (100 \times 72) \\
+\,2\,1\,6 \quad (3 \times 72) \\
\hline
7\,4\,1\,6
\end{array}
$$

AND STILL MORE BENEFITS

There's still another way in which the mental breakdown technique may be applied to many numbers. Let's see how we can use a new twist to get lightning-fast answers when multiplying by such numbers as 72 . . . 44 . . . 63 . . . 220 . . . 81 . . . 36 . . . and so on.

How? Well, look at this problem:

$$
\begin{array}{r}
6\,3\,2 \\
\times\ \ \ 3\,6 \\
\hline
\end{array}
$$

The multiplier, 36, can be seen as 40 – 4. (Remember about rounding off to obtain zeros?) Thus if we (1) multiply 632 by 40 (which is simply multiplying by 4 and adding a zero), and then (2) subtract 632 × 4 (same product or answer, without the zero) from our first product, we get the correct answer. Like this:

632 × 40 ----------------- 2 5 2 8 0

minus   632 × 4, or

1/10 of 632 × 40 (25280) ---- 2 5 2 8

2 5̸ 7 5̸ 2 —— 22752

Do you see how easy it is? A single calculation —
632 × 4 — was required to determine both products;
then one was subtracted from the other.

This should show you that any number that falls into
this category is a cinch to handle. I mean the "1/10th"
category. To simplify:

If you can raise or lower any number to one which
ends in zero; and if the amount which you added or took
away is 1/10 of the zeroed number — then two simple
calculations will solve an otherwise difficult multiplication problem for you.

Do you understand why? Look: if you add 8 to 72 to
get 80 — 8 is 1/10 of 80 — therefore it can be included
in the "1/10" category. Therefore, to multiply a number by 72, first multiply it by 80, and then subtract 1/10
of the product. In the same way, to multiply by 88; again
multiply by 80 — but this time add 1/10 of the product.

So, to multiply 936 by 88 — 936 × 80 (multiply by 8
and add a zero) is: 74880. 1/10th of that product (just
drop the zero) is 7488. Therefore, 74880 plus 7488 is
the same as 936 × 88. The answer, is 82368.

Now let's take another example. To multiply by 81,
you can see 81 as 90 minus 9. (9 is 1/10 of 90.) Multiply by 90 and then subtract 1/10 of that product. Follow?

This technique can just as easily be applied to larger
numbers, where it really becomes a great help. For
example:

6242 be-   4 9 9 3 6 0 0 — (6242 × 800; multiply by 8
    comes   and add two zeros.)
× 720   — 4 9 9 3 6 0 — (6242 × 80; 1/10 of the
                  4 ⁵0̸4 ⁵40   first product.)

                  4 4 9 4 2 4 0

And one more example, using a two-digit number:

7 1 2   becomes 4 9 8 4 0   (712 × 70)

× 7 7   + 4 9 8 4 — (712 × 7: 1/10 of first product)

                  5 4 8 2 4

LET'S COMPARE THE TWO METHODS

You've learned <u>two</u> different ways to simplify dozens of multiplication problems, and come up with lightning-quick answers.

<u>Both methods</u> tell you to take a number which involves hard multiplication, and break that number down into two easier numbers which you can calculate in your mind.

In the <u>first method</u>, you round out the number till it becomes easy to multiply (for example, 99 becomes 100). And then you simply subtract (or add) the original number from your product to get the correct answer.

(For example, in multiplying 432 × 99, first multiply 432 × 100 = 43,200. And then simply subtract 432 from your product — 43,200 − 432 = 42,768.)

In the <u>second method</u>, on the other hand, although you again round off the number till it becomes easy to multiply (77 becomes 70), in this case you subtract (or add) <u>a fraction of your product</u> to get the correct answer.

(For example, in multiplying 432 × 77, you first convert the 77 to 70. Then multiply 432 × 70 = 30,240. And then simply add 1/10 of that figure — or 3,024 — to that product. Thus 30,240 + 3,024 = 33,264.)

There you have your two techniques — ready to go to work for you.

Can some numbers be mentally broken down in either way? Yes! For example, 81 may be thought of as 90 times the number, minus 1/10 of the product.

Or, if you find it easier, 81 may be thought of as 80 times the number, plus the number.

Preference for one or the other of these formulas can depend on the number to be multiplied, or on your own preference.

So train yourself to see the breakdown possibilities in every number to be multiplied. For example, see if you can determine breakdown formulas for each of the following numbers.

DRILL NO. 2 IN MENTAL BREAKDOWN — BREAKING DOWN

1. 96 becomes 100 − 4	**11.** 45 becomes
2. 22 becomes 20 + 1/10	**12.** 51 becomes
3. 44 becomes 40 + 1/10	**13.** 55 becomes
4. 71 becomes 70 + 1	**14.** 49 becomes
5. 72 becomes 80 − 1/10	**15.** 18 becomes
6. 11 becomes	**16.** 270 becomes
7. 79 becomes	**17.** 199 becomes
8. 63 becomes	**18.** 27 becomes
9. 66 becomes	**19.** 69 becomes
10. 54 becomes	**20.** 19 becomes

Now, using the formulas which you've devised for simplifying these numbers, multiply each of them by 513.

⬜1.⬜   5 1 3   becomes   5 1 3 0 0   (513 × 100)
      × 9 6   − 2 0 5 2   (513 × 4)
                        4 9 2 4 8

⬜2.⬜   5 1 3   becomes   1 0, 2 6 0   (513 × 20)
      × 2 2   + 1 0 2 6   (1/10 of 10,260)
                        1 1, 2 8 6

Now do the rest yourself. And by the way, the multipliers do not necessarily follow the order of the quiz on Page 131.

3.
$$\begin{array}{r}513 \\ \times\ 44 \end{array}$$ becomes

4.
$$\begin{array}{r}513 \\ \times\ 71 \end{array}$$ becomes

5.
$$\begin{array}{r}513 \\ \times\ 72 \end{array}$$ becomes

6.
$$\begin{array}{r}513 \\ \times\ 79 \end{array}$$ becomes

7.
$$\begin{array}{r}513 \\ \times\ 63 \end{array}$$ becomes

8.
$$\begin{array}{r}513 \\ \times\ 66 \end{array}$$ becomes

9.
$$\begin{array}{r}513 \\ \times\ 54 \end{array}$$ becomes

10.
$$\begin{array}{r}513 \\ \times\ 45 \end{array}$$ becomes

11.
$$\begin{array}{r}513 \\ \times\ 51 \end{array}$$ becomes

12.
$$\begin{array}{r}513 \\ \times\ 11 \end{array}$$ becomes

13.
$$\begin{array}{r}513 \\ \times\ 55 \end{array}$$ becomes

14.
$$\begin{array}{r}513 \\ \times\ 49 \end{array}$$ becomes

15.
$$\begin{array}{r}513 \\ \times\ 18 \end{array}$$ becomes

16.
$$\begin{array}{r}513 \\ \times\ 270 \end{array}$$ becomes

17.
$$\begin{array}{r}513 \\ \times\ 199 \end{array}$$ becomes

18.
$$\begin{array}{r}513 \\ \times\ 27 \end{array}$$ becomes

19.
$$\begin{array}{r}513 \\ \times\ 69 \end{array}$$ becomes

20.
$$\begin{array}{r}513 \\ \times\ 19 \end{array}$$ becomes

LET'S REVIEW WHAT WE'VE LEARNED

Have you got the hang of it now? Do you understand exactly what I'm talking about when I tell you that ment-al breakdown can cut your multiplication labor to the bone? Let's give this technique one final going-over

What is mental breakdown? The exchange of a tough-to-do arithmetical process for one — or even two — easy steps. Instead of multiplying 87 × 99, multiply 87 × 100, then subtract 87. 8700 − 87 = 8613.

What is the purpose of using the mental breakdown technique? To simplify the actual computing that must be done, thereby reducing the possibility of error, and increasing speed. In many instances, the simplified computing can be done entirely in your head.

How do you apply mental breakdown to solve a prob-lem? By replacing one of the problem's multipliers. Instead of multiplying 367 × 90, you multiply it first by 100 and then subtract 10 × 367, or 1/10 of the product.

On what kind of numbers will mental breakdown work? Mental breakdown can simplify multiplication involving any number which can be "rounded off" to an easier-to-work-with number.

When is mental breakdown a genuine short cut? It's legitimate when you can quickly spot a good way to ex-change a difficult task for an easy one — or two easy ones. This way, you cut out 90% of your work — and al-most 100% of your errors.

Does it pay to try to find ways of breaking down every number? That's up to you. The thing to do is use mental breakdown when it comes to you easily. If it saves time and trouble, by all means use it.

And if you run into a problem that won't sit still for mental breakdown maybe you'll have better success with another short cut device. Maybe you'll see how to sim-plify the problem with the next supercharged technique you will learn — in the next chapter.

CHAPTER SIX

More Multiplication
Short Cuts

Now that you've seen how easy these miracle short cuts make hundreds of everyday multiplication problems, let's go on to learn a few more that make child's play of most business and budget multiplication.

"There's more than one way to skin a cat." — Old folk saying.

When you multiply $836 by 60, you naturally (by this time, I hope) multiply first by 6. And then — multiply that step's product, $5,016, by 10, simply by tacking a zero onto the end: $50,160.

But do you remember where and when you first learned to exchange one hard job for two simple ones in this way — using the formula of $60N = 6N \times 10N$?

It was in school, of course, that you first learned about that magic word <u>factors</u>! It was there that you learned that $18 \times \underline{4 \times 3}$ will produce the same answer as $18 \times \underline{12}$, because $\underline{4 \times 3} = \underline{12}$. Because 4 and 3 are the <u>factors</u> of 12.

As a matter of fact, since 6 and 2 are also factors of 12, you'll get the identical answer using $18 \times 6 \times 2$ or $18 \times 3 \times 4$, or 18×12. Here's the proof:

```
      1 8
    × 1 2
      1 8 6
        3
    1 1 6  =  2 1 6
```

```
      1 8                          1 8
    ×   4                        ×   6
      7 2                        1 0 8
    ×   3                        ×   2
    2 1 6                        2 1 6
```

So, instead of multiplying a number by 12, you could multiply by either one of its two factors — 4 × 3 or 6 × 2.

(In all these instances and examples, I'm using these numbers only for explanation purposes. We both know that to multiply by 12, you could just as easily use the formula 10 times the number plus 2 times the number. In this way, 18 × 12 = 180 (18 × 10) + 36 (18 × 2).

So now you can simplify the problem of multiplying by 12 with either of two "factor the matter" formulas — 12 times a number = 4 times the number times 3. Or 12 times a number = 6 times the number times 2.

A factor of a number is any smaller number that "goes into" it without leaving a remainder. Factors of 24 are 2, 3, 4, 6, 8, and 12.

2 goes into 24 twelve times, without a remainder. Therefore, 2 is a factor of 24.

3 goes into 24 eight times, without a remainder. Therefore, 3 is a factor of 24.

4 goes into 24 six times, without a remainder. There-fore, 4 is a factor of 24.

6 goes into 24 four times, without a remainder. Therefore, 6 is a factor of 24.

8 goes into 24 three times, without a remainder. Therefore, 8 is a factor of 24.

12 goes into 24 two times, without a remainder. Therefore, 12 is a factor of 24.

And you can factor the matter — using factors to simplify the work in multiplication — by using any two (or three or more) factors whose product is one of the multipliers. When exchanging a multiplier of 24 for factors, you may use 2 and 12, or 3 and 8, or 4 and 6. (But you can't use 4 and 8, because their product is not equal to 24 — the multiplier they replace.)

To multiply by a factorable number, multiply first by one factor, then multiply the result by the other factor. Instead of multiplying by 24, you can multiply successively by any combination of smaller numbers which, when multiplied together, produce 24 — 12 and 2 ... 8 and 3 ... 6 and 4 ... 4 and 3 and 2 ($4 \times 3 = 12$; $12 \times 2 = 24$). Watch:

37	37	37	37	37
× 24	× 12	× 8	× 6	× 4
648	374	246	182	128
12	6	5	4	2
12	1	296	222	148
888	444	× 3	× 4	× 3
	× 2	678	888	324
	888	21		12
		888		444
				× 2
				888

Do you understand exactly how this new short cut device works? Do you understand <u>why</u> it works? In order to be absolutely certain that nothing about the <u>factor the matter</u> device confuses you, let me try one more explanation.

The "Factor-the-Matter Device" allows you to substitute two or more easy-to-work-with numbers for a harder number. Thus, in multiplying 77 × 18, you simply multiply 77 first by 9, which equals 693, and then multiply this 693 by 2 to get your final answer, 1,386.

Is that clear? So long as the factors, when multiplied, equal the number they replace, your final product will be correct. Because all you've done is <u>regroup the units which make up that product.</u>

To prove this to yourself even more dramatically, work out the products of each of the following problems, now, using every set of factors which I suggest.

DRILL NO. 1 IN FACTOR-THE-MATTER
MULTIPLICATION

$\boxed{1.}$ 36 × 24 =

$\boxed{2.}$ 36 × 8 × 3 =

$\boxed{3.}$ 36 × 6 × 4 =

$\boxed{4.}$ 36 × 4 × 3 × 2 = $\boxed{7.}$ 24 × 6 × 6 =

$\boxed{5.}$ 36 × 3 × 2 × 2 × 2 = $\boxed{8.}$ 24 × 4 × 3 × 3 =

$\boxed{6.}$ 24 × 9 × 4 = $\boxed{9.}$ 24 × 3 × 3 × 2 × 2 =

NOW LET'S SEE HOW THIS DEVICE
MAKES TOUGH PROBLEMS EASY

So . . . that's how factors work, and that's more than enough proof that they <u>do</u> work. But just where does the <u>factor the matter</u> device save you time, work, and worry?

As simply as this! Do me a favor, please, and try to multiply 29 by 16 — mentally.

Having trouble? Well, now consider the fact that 16 is really $2 \times 2 \times 2 \times 2$. And now see if you can double 29 successively, four times! 29 . . . 58 . . . 116 . . . 232 . . . 464!

Are you convinced?

Using the factor-the-matter device when you must multiply mentally is one of the most dramatic demonstrations of the priceless advantages of modern mathematical short cuts. It is undeniably good sense to make the actual work you must do as simple as possible, and to take that work in the smallest individual doses you can manage. And that's what the factor-the-matter device can do for you, in countless multiplication situations.

WHEN CAN YOU FACTOR?

The next step in learning the factor-the-matter device is to discover how to determine whether a specific number is factorable.

You know the times-tables well by now, if you drilled in them as I instructed in Chapter 4. You should know them well enough so that when you look at 72 you know immediately that its factors are 9 and 8.

Between 4 and 81, there are dozens of numbers whose factors you will immediately recognize from your times-tables, and several others whose factors are easily recognizable — 33 (11×3) . . . 60 (20×3 or 30×2 or $5 \times 4 \times 3$) and so on.

But what about the rest of the infinite range of numbers which you can at any time be called upon to multiply?

You must be able to look at a number and know, fast, whether you will get any help with it from the factor-the-matter device. You must be able to determine, fast, whether a specific number is factorable, and by what digit or digits it is factorable. And you can, with a handful of simple clues. Here they are:

A number is factorable by 2 if its last digit is even. 2, 4, 6, 8, 10, 12, 100, 462, 464, 466, 1,002, 114, 628 ...

A number is factorable by 3 if the sum of its digits is divisible by 3. 3, 6, 9, 12 (1 + 2 = 3), 15 (1 + 5 = 6), 123, 609, 1,803, 4,824 . . . .

A number is factorable by 4 if its last two digits are divisible by 4, or if its last two digits are zeros. 4, 8, 12, 16, 112, 416, 908, 1,200, 148, 328 . . . .

A number is factorable by 5 if its last digit is a 0 or 5. 5, 10, 15, 20, 115, 870, 2,385, 4,117,005 . . . .

A number is factorable by 6 if its last digit is even and the sum of its digits is divisible by 3. 6, 12, 18, 24, 3,006, 7,914 . . .

There is a way to determine whether a number is factorable by 7; but it isn't worth the trouble . . . take my word for it.

A number is factorable by 8 if, after it is factored by 4, the other factor (we call the other factor a co-factor) is an even number. 8 (4 × 2), 16 (4 × 4), 24 (4 × 6), 32 (4 × 8), 152 (4 × 38), 2,936 (4 × 734), 38,584 (4 × 9,646) . . .

Do you follow that? 4 is a factor of each of these numbers. The other factor, or co-factor, in each case, is an even number. 828 would not be factorable by 8 because, although it is factorable by 4, the co-factor 207 (4 × 207 = 828) is not an even number.

A number is factorable by 9 if the sum of its digits — continuously added until reduced to a single digit — is 9. 9, 18 (1 + 8 = 9), 27 (2 + 7 = 9), 36 (3 + 6 = 9), 126 (1 + 2 + 6 = 9), 495 (4 + 9 + 5 = 18; 1 + 8 = 9), 6,381 (6 + 3 + 8 + 1 = 18; 1 + 8 = 9), 743,796 (7 + 4 + 3 + + 7 + 9 + 6 = 36; 3 + 6 = 9). (We call this remaining single digit — in all of these examples, the single digit 9 — the digital root.)

And of course you know without my telling you that any number ending in 0 is factorable by 10; any number ending in 00 is factorable by 100. Beyond that, there isn't much point in studying clues, since the job of dividing the number by the small factor to determine the other factor becomes too much trouble to make it worthwhile.

NOW LET'S START FACTORING

At any rate, those are all the clues you'll ever have to know to determine the factorability of a number, and here's how you'll use them.

For example, if you must multiply by 648, can you factor the matter?

Look for the largest factor you can find, because if it works it'll leave you with the smallest second factor. So begin your search for a factor by adding the number's digits.

$6 + 4 + 8 = 18$; $1 + 8 = 9$. 648 is factorable by 9; its co-factor ($648 \div 9$) is 72. That's a times-table product — 9×8. So the factors of 648 are 9, 9, and 8. $9 \times 9 \times 8 = 648$.

So, to multiply 342 by 648, you'd get the right answer if you multiplied 342 by 9 (3078); then 3078 by 9 (27702); and finally, 27702 by 8 — to arrive at 221616.

Try another one:

Are you aware that you needn't stop at 9 and 8 when you factor 72? $9 = 3 \times 3$, and $8 = 2 \times 2 \times 2$ — $72 = 3 \times 3 \times 2 \times 2 \times 2$!

Want to see how this information helps you? Can you multiply 72×51 in your head? Probably not. But now look at it this way: $51 \times 3 = 153$; $\times 3 = 459$; $\times 2 = 918$; $\times 2 = 1836$; $\times 2 = 3672$.

All right . . . now let's really go to work. Using the factor-the-matter technique, solve each of the problems in this

DRILL NO. 2 IN FACTOR-THE-MATTER
MULTIPLICATION

[1.]   3 2 4   [2.]   7 8 5   [3.]   6 8 1
       × 1 6   × 1 5   × 4 5

[4.]   6 8 6   [5.]   8 2 3   [6.]   4 9 8
       × 5 6   × 6 3   × 2 2

[7.]   4 9 3   [8.]   7 3 8   [9.]   9 3 6
       × 5 4   × 5 6   × 4 2

[10.]   5 8 6
       × 4 9

COMBINING DEVICES

If you stop to think about it for a moment, you're really quite versatile already, even with just these first two short–cut devices — mental breakdown and factor the matter. To demonstrate what I mean, back up a moment and take another look at that problem of 72 × 51.

You didn't have to use the factor-the-matter technique at all, if you didn't want to. Because 72 is 80 − 8. And the mental breakdown formula for multiplying by 72 would be 72 = 80N − 1/10 of the product. Therefore, 80 × 51 = 4080; 1/10 of that is 408; 4080 − 408 = 3672.

Or, you could have combined the two devices in several ways:

72 is 2 × 36. So double 51 to get 102. And change the 36 to 40 − 1/10 of the product. This gives you 40 × 102, which equals 4080 − 408 − 3672.

Do you understand how I used <u>both</u> the <u>factor-the-matter</u> and the <u>mental breakdown</u> devices in this last example? If you don't, study it until you do!

Or you could multiply 51 × <u>4</u> − 204. And exchange the remaining co-factor of 72 − <u>18</u> − for 20N − 1/10 of the product. This gives you 204 × 20 = 4080; minus 408 − 3672.

<u>Or</u> − you could consider the 51 as 50 + 1. And then, multiply 72 by 100 (7200); then divide by 2 (3600) and add the number once − 3672.

Do you see how these devices can work with one another to simplify your tasks in multiplication? In this next drill, I want <u>you</u> to decide which device or devices, if any, you'll use. (Try more than one way, if you see them, just for practice.)

DRILL IN SHORT-CUT MULTIPLICATION − FREE STYLE

1.	4 5	2.	9 9	3.	9 5
	× 2 7		× 4 8		× 4 9

4.	6 3	5.	5 8	6.	3 2 4
	× 4 2		× 3 6		× 4 8

7.	4 1 4	8.	1 4 4	9.	3 3 6
	× 8 1		× 5 4		× 3 2

10.	2 9 9
	× 2 4

ANOTHER NEW SHORT CUT

Let's move on now, to still another special device for saving time, work, and worry in multiplication. With the technique I'm about to describe, you'll be able to reduce your hard labor by up to two-thirds in a surprisingly large number of instances when you must have exact answers to difficult problems — plus countless situations where a quick but accurate estimate is what you're after.

Let me illustrate this dramatic new device — which will enable you to trade double- and triple-digit multiplication for short division — with an everyday example.

You needed a new bowling ball, so you decided to save quarters toward this goal. Every day you placed one 25¢ piece in a jar on the dresser, and after two months (February and March) you thought you might have saved enough. A quick check of the calendar told you that there were 59 quarters in the jar . . . how much is that in price-tag language?

Wait a second! Before you get out the pad and start multiplying 59 × 25, isn't there a simpler way? How many quarters are there in a dollar? Can't you divide by 4, since each group of 4 quarters represents a dollar?

$$\begin{array}{r} 14\ 3/4 \\ 4\overline{)59} \end{array}$$

Those 59 quarters add up to exactly $14.75. And you were able to figure that out without a scrap of paper, because you knew that 4 quarters make a dollar. A lot quicker, you've got to admit, than the calculation of 59 × 25.

Do you completely understand what happened in this example? Because 25 and 4 are factors of 100, and because it is easier to divide by 4 than multiply by 25, you were able to replace that multiplier with a new kind of formula — 25 = 100 divided by 4! 25 = 100 ÷ 4.

Now let's see how this fits in with the other devices you've learned:

1. In using the mental breakdown device, you replaced one of the multipliers with an easier-to-use formula of addition or subtraction: 99 = 100 − 1.

2. In using the factor the matter device, you replaced one of the multipliers with an easier-to-use formula of multiplication: 36 = 9 × 4.

3. And now, in this new device — let's call it easy-division (or decimal-factor) — you replace one of the multipliers with an easier-to-use formula of division: 25 equals 100 ÷ 4.

THE EASY-DIVISION DEVICE AT WORK

Now, how often can you use this easy-division device to save time and error? Every time you come across a problem with figures like these, for example:

50 is 1/2 of 100. So, instead of multiplying by 50, you can add a pair of 0's and divide by 2.

125 is 1/8 of 1,000. So, instead of multiplying by 125, you can add three 0's and divide by 8.

75 is 3/4 of 100. So, instead of multiplying by 75, you can multiply by 300, then divide by 4. (This is actually multiplying by 3/4. You multiply by the top number of the fraction, and divide by the bottom one.)

Here's a table of easy-division figures — all based on 1,000 for convenience — which I promise you'll find useful in a surprising number of multiplication problems. (Note that the figures marked with an asterisk (*) are only approximate: quite handy for rapidly obtaining accurate estimates; but not exact factors of 1,000, hence not to be used for figuring exact answers.)

THE EASY-DIVISION TABLE

111* — 1/9	375 — 3/8	667* — 2/3
125 — 1/8	400 — 2/5	714* — 5/7
143* — 1/7	428* — 3/7	750 — 3/4
167* — 1/6	444* — 4/9	778* — 7/9
200 — 1/5	500 — 1/2	800 — 4/5
222* — 2/9	555* — 5/9	833* — 5/6
250 — 1/4	571* — 4/7	857* — 6/7
286* — 2/7	600 — 3/5	875 — 7/8
333* — 1/3	625 — 5/8	889* — 8/9

HOW TO MAKE INSTANT ESTIMATES

First, let's consider the usefulness of this easy-division device for figuring estimates with a minimum of work.

Assume you want a quick estimate of the cost of a certain quantity of a product — or, how much material you need for a production job — or any other problem involving multiplication. You want this estimate quickly and accurately, and you want it with a minimum amount of work — preferably without using pencil and paper.

In order to make that quick estimate of any number multiplied by any other number, do this:

1. Select one of the multipliers in your problem, and determine which figure in the above table is nearest to it. (Don't worry if your multipliers aren't three-digit figures — the decimal points will all take care of themselves automatically. To find the nearest figure in the table to your multiplier, simply consider 111 — the first figure in the table — as 111, 1.11, 11.1, 1,110, or any other number using those digits. It's all the same to the easy-division device.)

2. When you've located the multiplier in the table, note the fraction which it equals. (111 = 1/9). Now, substitute that fraction for the multiplier.

3. Add as many 0's to the other multiplier as there are digits in the number you've changed to a fraction. (For example, if you're using 1/9 instead of 111, then add three zeros to the other figure.)

4. Now multiply by the fraction. That is, multiply by its numerator (top number), and divide by its denominator (bottom number). When the numerator is 1, all you need do is divide by the denominator. In this example, simply divide by 9.

That's all there is to it! And you've automatically insured the correct placement of the decimal point, by adding the proper amount of 0's to the other multiplier.

Incidentally, the closer the table-figure is to your original number, the more accurate your estimate will be. Here are some demonstrations of this fact in action:

$$\begin{array}{r} 8\ 6\ 4 \\ \times\ 3\ 3\ 5 \\ \hline \end{array}$$

The closest entry in the easy-division table to 335 is 1/3. 335 contains three digits, so tack three 0's onto 864, and multiply by 1/3, which means that you divide by 3 — like this:

$$\begin{array}{r} 2\ 8\ 8\ 0\ 0\ 0 \\ 3\overline{)\,8\ 6\ 4\ 0\ 0\ 0} \end{array}$$

288,000 is just an estimate, remember. However, since the actual answer to the problem is 289,440, your estimate is pretty darn close!

Now let's look at another problem:

$$\begin{array}{r} 4\ 2\ 3 \\ \times\ 7\ 8 \\ \hline \end{array}$$

The closest entry to 78 is 7/9. (On the table, I showed 778 as 7/9 of 1,000. So you can see that 78 would be close to 7/9 of 100.) Add two 0's — the number of digits in 78 — to 423, and multiply by 7/9.

$$4\,7\,0\,0 \times 7 = 32,900$$
$$9\overline{\smash{)}\,4\,2\,3\,0\,0}$$

The exact answer is 32,994. Pretty close again!

If you're interested only in a quick estimate, it isn't even necessary to work out the problem beyond the number of places you require for that estimate. I provided complete solutions to the problems above just to show you how they're done; most of the time you'll be able to arrive at your estimate without touching a pencil.

And all you need are the figures in the easy-division table. You already know several of them, I'll bet, from your school days. And just a few minutes of drilling will make most of the others as familiar to you as the times-table.

Turn back right now to the easy-division table. Read it over a few times. And then see if you can fill in the correct (or closest) fractions for the figures in this

DRILL ON THE EASY-DIVISION TABLE
FOR RAPID ESTIMATING

[1.] 250		**[2.]** 600			
[3.] 875	**[4.]** 375	**[5.]** 833			
[6.] 111	**[7.]** 800	**[8.]** 125			
[9.] 2.50	**[10.]** 87 1/2	**[11.]** 444			
[12.] 2,860	**[13.]** 714	**[14.]** .005			
[15.] 14.3	**[16.]** 333	**[17.]** $85.70			
[18.] 222	**[19.]** 1.11	**[20.]** 11.1			

How did you do? The most important figures in the
table — the ones which you <u>must</u> have at the tips of your
fingers — are the <u>exact</u> figures: 125 (1/8), 200 (1/5),
250 (1/4), 375 (3/8), 400 (2/5), 500 (1/2), 600 (3/5),
625 (5/8), 750 (3/4), 800 (4/5), and 875 (7/8). It's
much, much, <u>much</u> easier to divide by 8 <u>and</u> multiply
by 5, than it is to multiply by 625.

Study the table a bit more, if you're not completely
satisfied with your command of it, and then use it to
solve the problems in this next drill.

Remember, it's as simple as 1, 2, 3:

1. Select the figure in the table (by memory, if you
can) which is closest to one of the multipliers of your
problem, and note its fractional equivalent.

2. Add to the problem's other multiplier as many 0's
as there are digits in the first multiplier.

3. Multiply that figure — the second multiplier, with
the correct number of 0's tacked on — by the fraction
you selected from the table.

Go on, now — try it.

DRILL NO. 1 IN MULTIPLYING BY
THE EASY-DIVISION DEVICE

1.	376 ×250	**2.**	624 ×125	**3.**	24 × 5
4.	917 ×143	**5.**	846 ×833	**6.**	392 ×286
7.	824 ×749	**8.**	415 ×198	**9.**	12,546 × 888

10.   3,496
     × 874

NOW LET'S SEE HOW EASY IT IS TO
GET PRECISE ANSWERS — THIS EASY WAY!

Onward, now, to the further application of this amazing device for the solution of difficult problems requiring precise answers. Since precision is necessary, only those numbers in the easy-division table that are precise factors of 1,000 will be useful. Let me repeat those exact factors for you a third time:

125 — 1/8	400 — 2/5	625 — 5/8
200 — 1/5	500 — 1/2	750 — 3/4
250 — 1/4	600 — 3/5	800 — 4/5
375 — 3/8		875 — 7/8

That's all — honestly, that's all you need to know.
If you've got to multiply by any one of these numbers,
or any decimal form of any one of these numbers
(1.25; 875,000,000; .0075, etc.), just tack on as many 0's
as necessary to the other multiplier, and multiply by
the fraction in the table.

How do you know how many 0's to tack on? Just
count the digits in the number you're trading in for the
fraction. One 0 is added to the other multiplier for
every digit to the left of the decimal point in the number
you convert into a fraction.

It's all just so simple, so dramatic, that I can't re-
sist showing it off for you! Here are two more examples of this easy-division device in action:

1. Each one of 75 members of a knitting club uses
exactly 2,680 yards of yarn per year. What is the club's
total annual yarn intake?

Which is easier?

$$
\begin{array}{r}
2680 \\
\times\, 75 \\
\hline
142600 \\
450 \\
104 \\
3 \\
\hline
190000
\end{array}
\quad \text{or} \quad
$$

$$\frac{3}{4}\Big/\overline{268000} \times 67000 = 201,000$$

(There are two digits
in 75; add two 0's to
2680.)

190000 — 201,000 yds.

A round trip from Newark, N. J., to Buffalo, N. Y.,
and back measures 875 miles. What would be the distance traveled on this route by a man who commuted
every day for a year (not Leap Year)?

Which is easier:

```
      365
    × 875
    248055          or        7 ×  45625 = 319,375
    4420                      ─────────────    miles
    2132                      8 / 365000
      45
      13
    ─────────
    208375  — 319,375 miles
```

ᐟ Now that you've seen how it's done, here's some
more practice in using this remarkable short-cut device.
Refresh your memory of the figures in the easy-division
table, and then solve the problems in this

DRILL NO. 2 IN MULTIPLYING BY
THE EASY-DIVISION DEVICE

1.   1,184   2.   625   3.   984
    × 125   × 32   × 875

4.   375   5.   944   6. $24.88
    × 144   × 7.5   × 50

7. $37.50   8.   25   9.   88
    × 24   × 4   × 7 1/2

10.   4,977
    × 333 1/3

THE EASY-DIVISION DEVICE IN
COMBINATION WITH OTHER DEVICES

Now let's put our growing arsenal of multiplication
short cuts to work — in combination — to flash through
seemingly "impossible" problems.

For example, here's a demonstration of the easy-
division device in cahoots with the mental breakdown
device:

Multiply 3,568 by 126. The formula: $126N = 125N + N$.

$$3,568 \times 125 = \begin{array}{c} 1 \\ 8 \end{array} \Big/ \begin{array}{c} 446000 + 3568 = 449{,}568 \\ \overline{3568000} \end{array}$$

Do you see what happened here? Let me break it
down to simplify. Multiplying by 126 is the same as
multiplying by 125 and then adding the number once
$(125 + 1)$.

125 is equivalent to $1/8$. 125 has three digits — so,
$1/8 \times 3568000 = 446{,}000$. That's the product of 125
(or $1/8$) times 3568. Now simply add the number once.
$446{,}000 + 3568 = 449{,}568$.

Impressed? That's just half the story. Now take
a look at the easy-division device at work side by side
with the factor-the-matter device:

How would you compute $3{,}616 \times 1750$?

The formula: $1750N = 875N \times 2$.

$$3616 \times 1750 = 2 \times \underline{7} \times \begin{array}{c} 452000 \\ 8 \Big/ \overline{3616000} \end{array} = 904000 \times 7 = 6328000$$

Let me break this one down for you. Halving 1750
gives you 875. $7/8$ is the exact fractional equivalent of
875. Since you halved the multiplier, the answer, naturally, will be 2 times 7/8 of 3616. Therefore, the formula:
$1750 = 875 \times 2$.

875 has three digits; so you tack three 0's onto 3616. Now, divide 8 into 3,616,000 to get 452,000. Double that (multiply by 2) to get 904,000; and then multiply that by 7 — 6,328,000.

Here are some other ways in which you can make "hard" multiplication easy with these short cuts:

To multiply by: 760, apply the formula:

750N + 10N. (750 is 3/4)

To multiply by: 225, apply the formula:

250N – 1/10. (250 is 1/4)

To multiply by: 350, apply the formula:

250N + 100N. (250 is 1/4)

To multiply by: 150, apply the formula:

75N × 2. (75 is 3/4)

To multiply by: 560, apply the formula:

80N × 7. (80 is 4/5)

To multiply by: 2,401, apply the formula:

600N × 4 + N. (600 is 3/5)

If you really wanted to, you could devise a formula to convert every multiplier you ever come across into fodder for the easy-division device. But if the conversion doesn't result in less work, and if you don't see the short cut promptly, it isn't a short cut at all.

Now I want you to devise formulas for converting multipliers in the following multiplication problems to figures to which the easy-division device is applicable.

DRILL IN CONVERTING MULTIPLIERS
FOR THE EASY-DIVISION DEVICE

| 1. | 124 = | 2. | 275 = | 3. | 365 = |

| 4. | 385 = | 5. | 16 = | 6. | 175 = |

| 7. | 495 = | 8. | 2,625 = | 9. | 1,750 = |

| 10. | 55 = | 11. | 623 = | 12. | 1,875 = |

Now — using the formulas you constructed, multiply each of those numbers by 7,874.

For example: $7874 \times 124 = 125N - N =$

$7874000 \times 1/8 - 7874 = 976376.$

AND THEY KEEP ON COMING!

But I'm not yet finished with multiplication short cuts! There's still one more important device you should know!

This last "major" device (they're all "major" when you're facing problems on which they work) is sort of a distant relative to the factor-the-matter device, in that it involves simplification of one of the problem's multipliers through multiplication.

You'll find it especially handy when one of the multipliers in your problem ends in 5 or contains a fraction.

THE TEMPORARY DOUBLE

Tell me the answer to this problem:

6 2

× 3 5

Too much trouble for you to rattle off the answer to that one mentally? Well, then, how about this one:

$$62 \times 70$$

And <u>this</u> one: $2\,\overline{)\,4\,3\,4\,0}$

Unless yours is a most unusual head for figures, you found it much easier to perform both of those last two calculations than to multiply 62 by 35. As a matter of fact, I'll bet you could have done those two problems in your head!

Well . . . you <u>did</u> multiply 62 × 35, although first you made a minor alteration in the form of the problem. And you were able to make the alteration because 35 is 1/2 of 70. Watch:

$$35 \times 62 = \frac{70}{2} \times 62 = \frac{70 \times 62}{2}$$

First, you simply <u>doubled</u> one of the multipliers in order to change it into an easier-to-use figure. (It's simpler to multiply by 70 than by 35, because there's only one digit to worry about.)

But you can't just go around doubling multipliers indiscriminately, without somehow making up for it later. That's why I call this device the <u>temporary double</u> — you pay it back at the end of the problem.

<u>Doubling a multiplier results in a double-size product.</u> So in order to compensate, you cut the answer in half. 70 × 62 = 4,340, and 35 × 62 is just 1/2 of that — 2,170.

<u>To multiply by a figure which ends in 5, double the figure, perform the calculation, then divide the answer by 2.</u>

$$45 \times 18 = \frac{90 \times 18}{2} = 2\,\overline{)\,1\,6\,2\,0} = 810$$

As a matter of fact, I'm sure you realize that you can simplify this problem still further.

Here's how: Compensate for your double before you perform the multiplication. Cancel the 2 out of that fraction, by cutting the other multiplier in half!

$$45 \times 18 = \frac{90 \times 18}{2} = \frac{90 \times 9}{1} = 810$$

Watch how this extra timesaver for the temporary double device works on an even simpler problem:

$$25 \times 48 = \frac{50 \times 48}{2} = \frac{50 \times 24}{1} = 1,200$$

See how easy it is! To convert many multiplication problems to an easier-to-handle form, double one of the multipliers, and then cut either the other multiplier or the answer in half.

By doubling once and halving once at the same time, you're performing a pair of calculations that in the long run give you exactly the same answer you would have obtained had you worked out the problem in its original form. And if in so doing you alter the form of the problem so that it's easier to tackle, you've got a legitimate short cut going for you.

And it doesn't matter whether it's the doubled number or the halved number — or both — that makes your work simpler.

Look at these examples of "temporary doubling" —

$25 \times 18 = 50$ (25 doubled) $\times 9$ (18 halved).

$50 \times 9 = 450$. $75 \times 16 = 150 \times 8 = 1200$;

and so on.

In these cases both of the numbers in the problem were exchanged for numbers that were considerably easier to handle, by doubling and halving before performing the final multiplication.

Use the temporary double device to solve the problems in this

DRILL NO. 1 IN MULTIPLYING WITH THE TEMPORARY DOUBLE DEVICE

[1.]	35 × 18 =	**[2.]**	45 × 24 =
[3.]	55 × 36 =	**[4.]**	25 × 48 =
[5.]	375 × 16 =	**[6.]**	15 × 264 =
[7.]	55 × 644 =	**[8.]**	45 × 612 =
[9.]	35 × 248 =	**[10.]**	25 × 862 =

THE TEMPORARY DOUBLE AND FRACTIONS

I mentioned before that the temporary double device can be especially useful when one of the multipliers of a problem contains a fraction. Watch:

$$4 \ 1/2 \times 18 = 9 \times 9 = 81.$$

You simply doubled 4 1/2 to get 9, and then halved 18 to get 9 — leaving you with the simple times-table calculation of 9 × 9. Thus you eliminated the fraction entirely.

Now, the most important facet of this device's application to problems involving fractions is that just as you can double and divide by 2 (or halve the other multiplier) to compensate, you can triple and divide by 3, or multiply and divide later by any number, as long as you multiply and divide by the same number.

This makes the temporary double device (I called it temporary "double" just to have a convenient title) more versatile, because it can be called upon to simplify numbers containing just about any fraction.

$$369 \times 33 \ 1/3 = 123 \times 100 = 12,300$$

Here, you simply _multiplied_ the 33 1/3 by 3 to get rid of the 1/3 (the multiplication also got rid of practically all of this problem's work). Then you _divided_ the other multiplier by 3, and made the compensation right on the spot.

Get back to work, now. Figure the answers to these problems.

DRILL NO. 2 IN MULTIPLYING WITH THE TEMPORARY DOUBLE DEVICE

1. 33 1/3 × 48 =	**2.** 7 1/2 × 48 =	
3. 4 1/5 × 45 =	**4.** 4 1/2 × 24 =	
5. 25 × 666 =	**6.** 6 2/3 × 981 =	
7. 7 1/7 × 357 =	**8.** 75 × 316 =	
9. 6 1/4 × 480 =	**10.** 9 1/11 × 132 =	

WHAT DID I TELL YOU?

Before you tackle your final examination in short-cut multiplication, let's take one last look at what you've learned in these last two chapters:

1. With the _mental breakdown_ device, you exchanged complicated problems like 67 × 99 for elementary ones like 67 × 100 − 1 = 6700 − 67.

2. With the _factor the matter_ device you traded in 91 × 63 for 91 × 9 × 7.

3. With the _easy-division_ table committed to memory, and with your knowledge of how this device is used, you looked at problems like 4,328 × 125 and saw 8 /4,328,000.

4. With the _temporary double_ device you learned to solve 35 × 18 by seeing in its place 70 × 9. And you also learned to see 3 1/2 × 462 as 7 × 231.

But most important of all, you've learned how to examine a multiplication problem and decide which of the
many ways of attacking it will be fastest, easiest, and
most accurate.

Now, as a final review, let's look at a problem that
can be solved with any one of the four major short-cut
devices described in this chapter:

$$3\ 0\ 3\ \times\ 7\ 5$$

First: The mental breakdown device. That 303 can
be reduced to two simple-to-handle numbers. 303N =
300N + 3N; or, 300N + 1/100 of the product.

$$303 \times 75 = 300 \times 75\ (22500) + 225 = 22,725$$

Second: The factor-the-matter device. The 75 can
be simplified by a multiplication formula. 75N = 5N ×
3 × 5.

$$
\begin{array}{r}
3\ 0\ 3 \\
\times\ 5 \\
\hline
1\ 5\ 1\ 5 \\
\times\ 3 \\
\hline
4\ 5\ 4\ 5 \\
\times\ 5 \\
\hline
2\ 2,7\ 2\ 5
\end{array}
$$

Third: The easy-division device. In the easy-division
table, 75 corresponds to 3/4. So add two 0's (the number of digits in 75) to 303, and multiply by 3/4.

$$\frac{3}{4} \times \frac{7\ 5\ 7\ 5}{/\ 3\ 0\ 3\ 0\ 0} = 22,725$$

Fourth: The temporary double device. Quadrupling
is the key to simplifying this problem with the temporary double. Multiply 75 × 4 — 300. Then, multiply

303 × 300, (simply multiply by 3 and add two zero's)
and divide the answer by 4 to compensate for the
quadrupling.

$$303 \times 300 = 90,900 \qquad 4\,\overline{\smash{\big)}\,90900} = 22725$$

Which of these devices was the best to use in solving
this problem? That's hard to say. If you just happened
to know that 75 × 3 = 225, the mental breakdown device
might have been fastest for you. Or perhaps you knew
that 75 × 4 = 300; then the temporary double (quadruple,
in this case) might have been your best bet.

The point is this: the more short-cut devices you
know, and the better you know how to use each of them,
the faster you will be able to determine exactly how to
solve every problem you face. Every problem you will
ever try to solve will be a special case of its own. To
approach it with less than all of your knowledge of
mathematics would be to weaken your ability to solve it.

Always consider every problem from every angle!
That's pretty good advice in mathematics — and in life
as well.

I've tried to explain all the different short-cut devices. If you don't make sure you understand them all
— if you don't learn them well — you're short-changing
yourself. Knowing all of them will give you the tools to
solve almost any multiplication problem quickly, easily,
and with less chance of error. You're limited only by
your own imagination!

Decide which is the easiest way to solve these problems, and then solve them:

FINAL EXAMINATION IN MULTIPLICATION
WITH SHORT-CUT DEVICES

1.　　　88
　　×36

2.　　312
　　× 71

3.　　125
　　× 44

4.　　477
　　× 6 2/3

5.　　99
　　×38

6.　　49
　　×7.5

7.　　959
　　× 14 2/7

8.　　144
　　× 45

9.　　502
　　× 24

10.　　128
　　× 35

Mathematical Miracle Number Four—How To Divide Without Dividing ... And Without Errors

Just as you learned that multiplication can be regarded as a form of extended addition, you'll now see how long division can be performed as progressive subtraction. And you'll use the modern methods of multiplication and subtraction — that you've already learned — to eliminate frustration, mistakes, and practically all the torturous work of the old method of long division!

". . . indivisible, with liberty and justice for all."

— from the Pledge of Allegiance to the Flag of the United States of America

But it seems that when there is dividing to be done, there's no justice! Somehow it hardly seems worth all the work, all the trouble, all the frustration you have to go through to solve a problem in long division — the old way!

And what does that old-fashioned method of division involve? Just this:

Guessing what to write down as the first digit of the answer . . . then tediously multiplying, digit by digit, only to find that you guessed too high . . . then erasing the work you've done, and multiplying again . . . then subtracting the product and remembering (hopefully) to "bring down" the dividend's next digit . . . and then starting that whole frustrating process all over again.

But now there is a better way to do long division — a technique of solving complicated problems that is so elementary, so obvious, you'll wonder why you never thought of it yourself!

And this new technique is so revolutionary, so logically self-explanatory, that it's about to be introduced in elementary schools all over America! One day, quite possibly, it will supplant the long way of doing long division.

Yes — somebody did think that a simpler method of doing long division was worth searching for . . . and if you've ever had to figure how many shares of stock at 27 1/2 you could buy with your $440 —

$$
\begin{array}{r}
1\ 6 \text{ shares} \\
2\ 7\ 5\ 0\ \overline{/\ 4\ 4\ 0\ 0\ 0} \\
2\ 7\ 5\ 0 \\
\hline
1\ 6\ 5\ 0\ 0 \\
1\ 6\ 5\ 0\ 0
\end{array}
$$

. . . if you've ever had to determine what fraction of your $55.00 Christmas budget you could spend on gifts for each of the 18 people on your list —

```
          3 0 5 +
   1 8 / 5 5 0 0
          5 4
          1 0 0
            9 0
            1 0
```

. . . if you've ever wanted to know how many miles your car was getting to the gallon when you drove 2,024 miles and used 88 gallons —

```
            2 3
   8 8 / 2 0 2 4
       1 7 6
          2 6 4
          2 6 4
```

then you'll agree wholeheartedly with the man who finally came up with that simpler method!

LET'S START BY NAMING A FEW NAMES

I'm going to need "handles" — names for the different components of a division problem — in order to properly explain this new method of doing long division.

It would be inconvenient to keep saying "the part that goes into the other part" and "the number you're dividing by the other number" . . . so let's name those parts before we get any deeper into the subject.

If the problem is to divide 15 by 3, we'll call 3 the divisor and 15 the dividend.

3 — the part that goes into, that does the dividing, is called the divisor.

15 — the part that stays put — that is being divided —
is called the dividend.

These are the traditional names for the components.

And the answer — 5, in this case — is sometimes
called the quotient, although we can just as conveniently
call it the answer.

The answer is the quotient. The divisor goes into the
dividend and produces the quotient.

The dividend is divided by the divisor, and produces
the quotient.

Okay? Okay. From now on, you'll see any division
problem like this:

$$5 \leftarrow \text{answer or quotient}$$
$$\text{Divisor} \leftarrow 3 \overline{\smash{)}1\,5} \leftarrow \text{dividend}$$

WHAT DIVISION REALLY IS

Take another look at that problem of 15 divided by 3.
Let's say that there are 15 singers, and whenever 3 of
them get together that makes another trio.

So what's the logical way to determine how many
trios can be formed from 15 singers? As simple as
this: First take 3 singers, give them a guitar, and send
them to Studio 1.

From the remaining 12 singers, take another trio
and send them to Studio 2.

Keep sending new trios to new studios until you run
out of singers, then count the occupied studios to see
how many trios you formed from the original 15 singers.

You've filled 5 studios, so 15 ÷ 3 = 5.

If you had started with 16 singers, you'd have formed
5 trios and you'd still have 1 singer left. He'd be the
remainder.

Now, what does all this really mean? Simply that
division is the process of determining how many little
bunches are contained in a big bunch. How many times
the divisor can be contained within the dividend. (How
many 3's in 15?) How many times the divisor can be
taken out of the dividend. And what's left over, if anything.

Just as multiplication is a sort of progressive addition, division is a sort of progressive subtraction.

Yes, division is progressive subtraction: Take as
many divisors (3's) away from the dividend (15) as you
can, and then count the number of divisors you've taken
away (5). That number will be the quotient — the answer.

That's the secret of this new method of doing division,
and the method itself is as logical, as elementary, as
magnificently obvious as the explanation. This is how
it looks when we start to use it:

$$3 \,/\,\overline{1\ 5}$$

This is the standard format for a division problem,
with just an extra vertical line hung onto the right end
(you'll understand why in just a moment). But first,
suppose you tell me how many times you think 3 goes
into — or, can be taken out of — 15. 5? All right, watch:

$$3 \,/\,\overline{1\ 5}\ \ 5$$
$$\underline{1\ 5}$$
$$0$$

Now, what did I do here? This:

1. I put down the 5 you gave me to the right of the
vertical line (that vertical line is there just to provide
a column for recording how many times I've removed
the 3).

2. Then I multiplied the divisor (3) by the number of times I removed it (5), and I wrote the product (15) below the dividend. (I know this is a short division problem, and anyone could have done it blindfolded. But be patient for a second, and you'll see where I'm going.)

3. There was no remainder when I subtracted the product (15) from the dividend (15), so the answer is 5.

But remember — I arrived at the answer by subtracting 5 groups of 3 from 15. Again, division is nothing more than progressive subtraction.

Now, in this example, because I knew that 3 went into 15 exactly 5 times, I finished the entire problem in one step. But suppose that when I asked you how many times you thought 3 went into 15, you told me 4. Would this complicate the problem? Not at all! Watch:

First I wrote the 4 to the right of the line. Then I multiplied the divisor (3) by the number of times I had removed it from the dividend (4). And then I subtracted my product of 3 × 4, or 12, to discover that I still had 3 left over.

Now — the only remaining question is: how many times does 3 go into 3?

$$3\,/\,\overline{1\ 5}\quad 4$$
$$\underline{1\ 2}$$
$$\overline{3}\quad 1$$
$$\underline{3}$$
$$5$$

3 goes into 3 once, of course. So I again wrote my 1
to the right of the vertical line. Then I multiplied 1 × 3
to get 3. And then simply subtracted that 3 from the 3
I had left over from the first step.

That time I <u>didn't</u> finish the problem in a single step;
so I took another step. Then, all I had to do was count
the distance I had progressed in both steps — by adding
the two numbers to the right of the vertical line — 4 + 1.

I could have done the problem in five separate steps
if I wanted to — or if I didn't know better. I could have
subtracted one 3 at a time from 15, and I'd still have
ended up with the same answer: 15 ÷ 3 = 5.

NOW LET'S REALLY PUT THIS
SHORT CUT TO WORK

I don't think that the picture of <u>what division is</u> could
be painted any more clearly than that. So let's move on,
now, and see how this method tears the <u>old</u> long-division
rule book to shreds.

If you were asked how many times you thought that
12 went into 876, you might make an off-the-top-of-your-
head guess of 70. A fifth-grade student might guess 50;
a less-schooled youngster might stab at the question with
a guess of 20.

Using the modern technique of treating division as
the progressive subtraction it really is, <u>all three of you</u>
would arrive at the same correct answer:

If you guessed 70:	If you guessed 50:	If you guessed 20:

```
If you              If you              If you
guessed 70:         guessed 50:         guessed 20:

12/876 | 70        12/876 | 50        12/876 | 20
 840   |            600   |            240   |
 ─────              ─────              ─────
  36   |  3         276   | 20         636   | 20
  36   |            240   |            240   |
 ─────              ─────              ─────
   0   | 73          36   |  3         396   | 20
                     36   |            240   |
                    ─────              ─────
                      0   | 73         156   | 10
                                       120   |
                                      ─────
                                        36   |  3
                                        36   |
                                       ─────
                                         0   | 73
```

See how easy it is! See how you never have to go
back, correct a mistake, and start all over again! You
just can't miss with this new method.

But before I turn you loose on some problems that
you can try on your own, I want to forewarn you of two
small kinks in this new technique that we'll iron out before seeing for yourself how this modern method works,
so I'll suggest two in-the-meantime alternatives — which
will, I promise, be eliminated by the time you've mastered this technique.

First, you might find that you're in hot water if any
of your guesses are <u>too high</u>. I'm going to eliminate
this kink in another page or two with one simple rule;
but in the meantime, guess low. If you're not sure
whether 12 goes into 876 70 times, guess 60. It won't
hurt to take an extra step or two the first time out.

Second, things could get a little complex when you
try to multiply a large divisor by an equally large num-

ber you guessed (for example 46 by 800). I'll soon show
you how to eliminate all difficulty along this line too.
But for now, if you can't see the product immediately
with one of your multiplication short-cut devices, work
it out on the side, on a piece of scrap paper. Okay?
Here's your first

DRILL IN LONG DIVISION THE
PROGRESSIVE SUBTRACTION WAY

[1.] $18\overline{/744}$ [2.] $24\overline{/936}$

[3.] $31\overline{/6,851}$ [4.] $29\overline{/2,407}$

[5.] $103\overline{/1,236}$ [6.] $448\overline{/167,552}$

[7.] $13\overline{/5,473}$ [8.] $92\overline{/2,116}$

[9.] $295\overline{/87,025}$ [10.] $16\overline{/252}$

YOU'VE GOT THE SECRET. NOW
LET'S ELIMINATE THE KINKS

How'd you like it? Did you notice how your answer
became progressively accurate — how with every subtraction you came closer and closer to having nothing
for a dividend?

Now let's get on to the business of ironing out those
kinks.

FIRST KINK: How to keep your first guess from
going too high. Obviously, you can't subtract more than

there is to take away, and that means you've got to keep your first estimate from being too high — and yet high enough so you need take only the least amount of steps. So here's a simple rule that lets you guess as close as possible without going too high.

For instance, take this problem:

$$2\,7\,\overline{\smash{\big)}\,6\,0\,7\,2}$$

Here's what you do:

Divide the dividend's first digit (or digits) by the first digit of the divisor, PLUS ONE. (2 + 1 = 3). So you divide 6 by 3 — which is about 2.

Then you tack on as many 0's as there are more digits in the dividend (6072 = four digits) than in the divisor (27 = two digits). So you add two zeros to your 2 to get 200. That's your first estimate, and it goes to the right of the vertical line, like this:

$$2\,7\,\overline{\smash{\big)}\,6\,0\,7\,2}\,\bigg|\,2\,0\,0$$
$$\underline{5\,4\,0\,0}\,\bigg|$$

Want to try it again? Then let's divide 955 by 33.

Again, you determine your first "guess" by increasing the divisor's first digit by one — 33 is the divisor, and the first digit plus one makes 4.

Then you divide the dividend's (955) first digit — 9 — by the 4; it goes about 2 times.

And then you see that there's one more digit in the dividend (955) than there is in the divisor (33), so you tack one zero onto that 2. And your first guess should be 20.

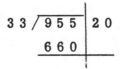

What you're doing, in effect, is estimating how many times 40 — rather than 33 — goes into the dividend. In this way, you make <u>sure</u> not to guess too high.

Of course, in some cases, this will give you a too-low estimate — but that creates no problem, whereas a too-high estimate does.

The only tricky part is determining how many zero's to tack on to your estimate, so let's spend some time looking at that.

We'll start with the simple cases: those where the first digit of the dividend is <u>larger</u> than the first digit of the divisor.

If the divisor is a two-digit number and the dividend is a three-digit number, tack on one 0.

If the divisor is a two-digit number and the dividend is a four-digit number, tack on two 0's.

If both the divisor and the dividend are two-digit numbers, don't tack on <u>any</u> 0's.

WATCH OUT NOW!

But now we butt up against the seemingly "hard" cases: those where the first digit of the divisor equals or exceeds the first digit of the dividend — 387 ÷ 48, for instance.

If you increase the first digit of the divisor (4) by 1, you've got a 5; and no matter how hard you push, you can't divide a 5 into a 3 (the first digit of the dividend). So, naturally, you estimate how many times 5 goes into 38 — the first <u>two</u> digits of the dividend.

Now, in order to determine how many 0's to tack on, you must consider the 38 as though it were a single digit. This means that since the divisor has two digits and the dividend also (for this purpose only) has two digits, you don't tack on any 0's. Watch:

```
4 8 / 3 8 7 | 7
      3 3 6 |
        5 1 | 1
        4 8 |
          3 | 8
```

387 ÷ 48 = 8, with a remainder of 3.

Now, if you hadn't counted the first two digits of the dividend as one digit when you figured how many 0's to tack on, you'd have ended up with an answer of 80.

The rule, then, is this:

If the divisor's first digit equals or exceeds the dividend's first digit, simply reduce by one the number of 0's you'd ordinarily tack on to your answer.

For example, say you are dividing 43,742 by 57. You realize that 6 (first digit of divisor + 1) won't go into 4, so you put it into 43 — the dividend's first two digits. And then you add only two 0's, since you regard the 4 and the 3 as a single digit when determining how many 0's to tack on. Therefore, your first guess is 700, not 7,000.

Now use this new rule to determine your first estimate only in the problems in this

DRILL NO. 1 IN ESTIMATING QUOTIENTS

Don't bother to solve these problems entirely, for now; simply make your first estimates of the quotients' first digits. And record the correct number of zero's, as well.

[1.] $324\overline{)23,976}$ [2.] $322\overline{)2,898}$

[3.] $93\overline{)5,952}$ [4.] $624\overline{)242,112}$

[5.] $367\overline{)87,923}$ [6.] $13\overline{)43}$

[7.] $47\overline{)18,753}$ [8.] $22\overline{)149}$

[9.] $36\overline{)7,276}$ [10.] $123\overline{)456,789,000}$

ONE MORE CAUTION

That should take care of kink number one, except for one last little suggestion. Since — in <u>any</u> problem — you'll have to <u>add up</u> your successive estimates in order to arrive at your answer, you'll want their digits to be properly arranged in columns, so it's impossible to make a mistake.

Therefore, your estimates should look like

<table>
<tr><th>this:</th><th>not this:</th></tr>
</table>

6 0 0	6 0 0
5 0	5 0
3 0	3 0
4	4

Toward this end, you'd be wise to determine the number of 0's you'll have to tack onto each estimate before recording it. Do it this way:

$$7\,6\,\big/\,\overline{3\,,8\,3\,2}$$

7 (the divisor's first digit) equals or exceeds 3 (the dividend's first digit). So I count the dividend's digits as 3-8, 3, and 2 — only three digits, for this purpose only. Since the divisor contains two digits, I record a single 0 outside the line, leaving space in front of it, like this:

$$7\,6\,\big/\,\overline{3\,,8\,3\,2}\,\big|\;\;0$$

Then, in front of that 0, I write the number of times that 8 (one more than the divisor's first digit) goes into 38 (the dividend's first two digits) — 4. Therefore, my first estimate is 40, like this:

$$7\,6\,\big/\,\overline{3\,,8\,3\,2}\,\big|\;\;4\,0$$

Using this modification of the basic rule, determine the first estimates only for the problems in this

DRILL NO. 2 IN ESTIMATING QUOTIENTS

[1.] $84\,/\,395$

[2.] $427\,/\,24,221$

[3.] $79\,/\,46,002$

[4.] $79\,/\,4,602$

[5.] $79\,/\,462$

[6.] $829\,/\,572,624$

[7.] $49\,/\,100$

[8.] $387\,/\,21,847$

[9.] $83\,/\,124,429$

[10.] $19\,/\,103$

NOW LET'S LICK THAT SECOND KINK

When your divisor is 46 and your estimate is 800, you're going to have trouble if you try to multiply those two numbers in your head. So iron out this kink by multiplying those two numbers on paper — but outside of your problem!

That's actually what I asked you to do before, but now I'm going to show you a perfect location for your calculations. Here's what they should look like:

```
46 / 3 9 4 2 2 | 8 0 0    3 2 8 0 0 (this is 800 × 46)
    3 6 8 0 0 |                4
      3̶ 6 2 2 |
```

First, to the immediate right of the estimate (which was determined by putting 5 into 39 and tacking on just two 0's because the divisor's first digit is larger than the dividend's), you simply perform left-to-right multiplication, as you learned back in Chapter 4.

You don't even have to count how many digits over to record the times-table products; all you have to do is put in the correct number of 0's: the same number as you tacked onto the estimate! (For example, here you simply multiply 46 × 8; then hook on two zeros.)

Now, as your second step, you transpose the sum of your multiplication-table products back into the problem, and subtract the product from the original dividend. This leaves you with the new dividend.

Here's how the rest of this problem works itself out:

```
46 / 3 9 4 2 2 | 8 0 0       3 2 8 0 0
    3 6 8 0 0   |               4
      ----------
      3̸ 6 2 2   | 5 0         2 0 0 0
    2 3 0 0     |               3
      ----------
        3 2 2   | 6           2 4 6
        2 7 6   |               3
      ----------
          4 6   | 1
          4 6   |
      ----------
            0   | 8 5 7
```

Here's another long division problem, worked out in the progressive subtraction manner. Follow each step. See if you can tell how each number in this problem was calculated.

```
3 5 6 / 8,4 8 2,4 1 2   2 0 0 0 0      0 6 0 2 0 0 0 0
        7 1 2 0  0 0 0                      1 1
        1 3 6 2  4 1 2   3 0 0 0        0 9 5 8 0 0 0
        1 0 6 8  0 0 0                      1 1
          2 9 4  4 1 2     7 0 0        2 1 5 2 0 0
          2 4 9  2 0 0                      3 4
           4 5  2 1 2     1 0 0
           3 5  6 0 0
            9  6 1 2       2 0
            7  1 2 0
            2  4 9 2         7
            2  4 9 2
                 0 | 2 3,8 2 7
```

NOW LET'S REVIEW LONG DIVISION

Division is nothing more than progressive subtraction, in which the answer to a problem tells how many times a divisor can go into a dividend. Since this is so, it's possible to determine the answer of a long division problem by subtracting the divisor, one bunch at a time, from the dividend, until there's nothing (or a number lower than the divisor, which would be the remainder) left.

Take two typical problems:

$$39\overline{)9437} \quad \text{and} \quad 39\overline{)2164}.$$

When estimating how many times the divisor should be subtracted on any given step, it's best to:

1. Increase the divisor's first digit (3) by 1 (to get 4), and see how many times that number goes into the dividend's first digit. (In the first problem, the divisor's first digit is 9. So 4 goes into 9 <u>two</u> times.)

2. Using that number (2) as the first digit of the estimate, tack on to it as many 0's as there are more digits in the dividend than the divisor. (In the first problem, there are four digits in the dividend, and two digits in the divisor. Therefore, you tack on two zeros to get 200 as your estimate.

3. If the divisor's first digit is as large as, or larger than, the dividend's (such as the second problem, where 3 is larger than 2), divide the dividend's first <u>two</u> digits by the divisor's first digit plus one (21 divided by 4, to get 5), and tack on one less 0 than would have otherwise been called for (instead of tacking on two zeros, you add only one — to get an estimate of 50).

Always use the times-table-products method of multiplying to determine the product of the estimate and divisor; the paperwork is done to the right of the estimate. Subtract that product from the dividend. And then repeat the process as many times as it's necessary to reduce the dividend to 0 or to a number less than the divisor. If there is a number less than the divisor, it's a remainder.

Do you understand all of this? With just a bit of practice you'll soon get the hang of it; and your growing number-sense and familiarity with this process will soon have you dividing even huge numbers in seconds.

YOUR FINAL EXAM IN PROGRESSIVE-
SUBTRACTION DIVISION

[1.] $324\overline{)23,976}$ [2.] $322\overline{)2,898}$

[3.] $93\overline{)5,952}$ [4.] $624\overline{)242,112}$

[5.] $367\overline{)87,923}$ [6.] $13\overline{)43}$

[7.] $47\overline{)18,753}$ [8.] $22\overline{)149}$

[9.] $36\overline{)7,276}$ [10.] $123\overline{)456,789,000}$

REVIEW QUIZ NO. 4

If you can't answer <u>all</u> these questions, go back to
the beginning of this chapter and review the sections
that you haven't fully understood. Remember, the only
acceptable mark is 100%.

[1.] What part of the conventional method of
      long division causes confusion, wasted
      time and errors?

      Why?

[2.] How has this been cured in this chapter?

[3.] How does the system for estimating quotients assure that you never estimate too high?

[4.] Why is long division really progressive subtraction?

[5.] In the modern way of doing long division, does it matter if you estimate too low?

Why?

[6.] In estimating the first quotient for this problem: 38/2437214   how many zeros would you tack onto the 6?

Why?

[7.] Do you thoroughly understand and grasp all the techniques taught in this chapter?

ANSWERS

[1.] Estimating how many times the divisor goes into the dividend.

Because this is usually an entire long division problem in itself.

[2.] By teaching you a system for calculating these quotients.

[3.] By making you add 1 to the first digit of the divisor.

[4.] Because its simply a matter of finding out how many times the divisor can be subtracted from (taken out of) the dividend.

[5.]   No.

Because it only necessitates an extra
simple step or two — still bringing
you to the correct answer.

[6.]   Four zeros. (60000)

Because you divided 4 (first digit of the
divisor plus 1) into the first two digits of
the dividend. Therefore those first two
digits are considered as one digit. Con-
sequently, for our purposes, there are
four more digits in the dividend than in
the divisor.

[7.]   Yes.

If you weren't able to answer these questions correctly and completely, you'd better reread this chapter
until you can — until you feel you really and thoroughly
understand all the techniques involved.

CHAPTER EIGHT

Short-Cut Devices And Techniques For Gaining Even Greater Speed In Division

The short-cut devices which you learned for simplifying subtraction and multiplication can be easily adjusted and adapted to speed you through countless division problems. Here's how:

"Divide and conquer . . . ."

— Ancient Roman saying

Just as there are special short cuts that can save you work in many specific problems involving addition, subtraction and multiplication, so there are special devices which can rip into the work you must perform to solve many long-division problems.

FIRST BY USING THE TRICKS YOU'VE JUST LEARNED

For example, take the modern technique of multiplication and subtraction that you learned in the earlier chapters of this book. They alone will prove to be tre-

mendous work-eliminators when you turn them loose
on the intermediate steps and calculations in long-division problems.

Just look at the time the decimal factor (or easy-
division) short-cut will save you in this problem, as you
attempt to multiply the divisor and your first estimate:

$$24 \, \overline{/ \, 1\,5\,0\,4\,8} \, \Big| \, 5\,0\,0$$
$$\underline{1\,2\,0\,0\,0} \Big|$$

$$5\,0\,0 \times 2\,4 = 1/2 \times 2\,4 \times 1\,0\,0\,0 = 1\,2\,0\,0\,0$$

(If you're not sure of this, check the decimal
factor system in chapter 6.)

Over and over again, you'll find yourself quickly
seeing opportunities to apply such short-cut multiplication devices. And you quickly calculate your multipli-
cations by adding nothing more than simple times-table
products.

And, at the same time, the one-second slash technique
will enable you to subtract those products as quickly
as you can write them down:

$$3\,6 \, \overline{/ \, 3\,2\,4\,7\,2} \, \Big| \, 8\,0\,0$$
$$\underline{2\,8\,8\,0\,0} \Big|$$
$$\cancel{1}\,\cancel{4}\,6\,7\,2 \Big|$$

THEN BY LEARNING SOME
BREATH-TAKING NEW TRICKS

But many long-division problems can be simplified
much, much further — even beyond the extent to which

our modern methods have already eliminated most of the work — through the use of various short-cut devices "custom tailored" to fit division problems that have specific features.

It's not surprising, really, that the short cuts most frequently useful in simplifying problems of long division are variations of the same you've learned to use so effectively in multiplication. The process of division — which you've learned to regard as progressive subtraction — is the reverse process to multiplication — which you've learned to regard as extended addition.

So the very short-cut devices which proved so effective in simplifying multiplication problems need only be converted — turned inside out, so to speak, to be every bit as effective in the simplification of long division.

THE MENTAL BREAKDOWN DEVICE IN LONG DIVISION

The mental breakdown device, for example, simplifies the work of long division in many ways.

1. Its application in the process of subtraction — which you can review, if necessary, by rereading the appropriate section of Chapter 4 — can speed up the time it takes you to subtract the products of long division's progressive estimates, like this:

$$37\overline{)345}8$$
$$\phantom{37\overline{)}}296$$
$$\phantom{37\overline{)}}\underline{}$$
$$\phantom{37\overline{)2}}49$$

becomes

$$345 - 296 = 349 - 300 = 49$$

You simply added 4 to each number, to bring one of them to a zero.

2. <u>Mental breakdown</u> can simplify many short-division problems to the point where there's no adding, subtracting, or multiplying to perform. . . and the answer pops out automatically.

Consider, for example, the problem of 36,459 ÷ 9. Stated as a <u>mental breakdown</u> formula, the problem looks like this:

$$36,459 \div 9 = \frac{36,000 + 450 + 9}{9} =$$

$$\frac{36,000}{9} + \frac{450}{9} + \frac{9}{9}$$

Watch how the problem can be done so that the answer pops out automatically:

$$9\overline{\smash{)}36,459} \ \bullet\bullet\bullet \ 9\overline{\smash{)}36}^{\ \ 4} \quad 9\overline{\smash{)}45}^{\ \ 05}$$

$$9\overline{\smash{)}9} \ \bullet\bullet\bullet \ 4,051$$

The individual answers of those individual problems represent portions of the over-all answer.

Simple enough? Now — to give you better insight into how this device works to simplify <u>dozens</u> of division problems you run into every day, I'm going to ask you to use <u>mental breakdown</u> to solve the problems of this

DRILL IN DIVIDING WITH
MENTAL BREAKDOWN

$[1.]$ $8\,/\,3\,2\,8$ $[2.]$ $2\,4\,/\,7,2\,4\,8$

$[3.]$ $9\,/\,6\,3,9\,5\,4$ $[4.]$ $1\,5\,/\,7\,5,0\,1\,8$

$[5.]$ $1\,2\,/\,3\,6\,1,2\,4\,8$

SIMPLIFYING LONG DIVISION WITH
THE FACTOR-THE-MATTER DEVICE

Instead of starting off with a detailed discussion of this device's application in long division, let me just quickly point to the fact that 4 and 3 are factors of 12, and then immediately show you a couple of solutions to a long-division problem:

	The Usual Way		The Factor-the-Matter Way
$12\,/\,3864$		3 0 0	3 2 2
3 6 0 0			$3\,/\,966$
	2 6 4	2 0	$4\,/\,3864$
	2 4 0		
	2 4	2	
	2 4		
	0	3 2 2	

The example on the left is the result of solving this problem by means of the progressive subtraction technique which you learned in Chapter 7. I even used a short cut of a sort when my natural number-sense told me that my first estimate could be 300 (rather than 100, which the regular method of estimating would have dictated), since 12 could obviously go into 38 at least 3 times.

But even with the saving in work which that solution represented over the conventional long-division process, it didn't even come close to what the factor-the-matter device did to this long-division problem!

All I had to do was divide the dividend by one of the factors of the divisor, then divide the answer of that short division calculation by the divisor's other factor. Two simple problems in short division, instead of a lengthy exercise in multiplying and subtracting!

Do you see how the factor-the-matter device is applied in the solving of long division problems? Turn the problem around, into a multiplication example, for a closer look. If $3,864 \div 12 = 322$, then we can say — just for the purpose of seeing this process in cross-section — that $322 \times 12 = 3,864$.

Look at 322×12 and decide how to produce its answer with the help of the factor-the-matter device. Since 12 can be factored into 4 and 3, you'd multiply first by 3 — $322 \times 3 = 966$ — and then multiply that product (966) by 4: $966 \times 4 = 3864$.

You needn't stop at two steps in the factor-the-matter device when you use it to simplify division. Just as you learned to reduce multipliers to as many easy-to-use factors as needed, you can also reduce large divisors into a series of smaller numbers — by using the set of clues to factorability shown in Chapter 6.

Here's how it works in long division, on the problem of 217,728 ÷ 288:

$$288 \overline{)217,728}$$

288 is divisible by 8 — its factors are 8 and 36. (8 × 36 = 288)

But 36 is a times-table product — it's factors are 6 and 6.

Therefore, the factors of 288 are 8, 6, and 6. (While those factors could be reduced still further, it isn't necessary, since each is a single digit and requires no greater work than short division.) Now watch:

$$\begin{array}{r} 756 \\ 6 \overline{)4536} \\ 6 \overline{)27216} \\ 8 \overline{)217728} \end{array}$$

Use your knowledge of the factorability of numbers to break the divisors of the following problems into easy-to-use factors, and work out the correct answers. (It might be worthwhile to reread the appropriate section of Chapter 6 to refresh your memory for factoring numbers.)

DRILL IN DIVIDING WITH THE
FACTOR-THE-MATTER DEVICE

[1.] $36\overline{)792}$ [2.] $45\overline{)14{,}310}$

[3.] $24\overline{)10{,}488}$ [4.] $72\overline{)1{,}368}$

[5.] $49\overline{)1{,}666}$ [6.] $35\overline{)30{,}660}$

[7.] $21\overline{)26{,}187}$ [8.] $42\overline{)1{,}554}$

[9.] $192\overline{)2{,}688}$ [10.] $336\overline{)2{,}352{,}672}$

SIMPLIFYING LONG DIVISION WITH
THE EASY-DIVISION DEVICE

The easy-division device is every bit as useful for solving long-division problems as it is in simplifying complex multiplication problems. And for determining quick estimates, the decimal-factor table in Chapter 6 can be just as effectively used in division as in multiplication.

To convert the easy-division device into a useful tool for division, simply reverse the procedure. Instead of adding 0's to the multiplier (the procedure in using this device for multiplication), you move the dividend's decimal point to the left as many places as there are in the divisor. (If you are dividing by 25, for instance, which has two digits, you'd simply move the decimal

point in the dividend two places to the left. For example, 281,300 would become 2813.00.)

And instead of multiplying by the fraction which you
locate in the table, you divide by that fraction — or
multiply by the fraction turned upside down!

For example, as you now know, to multiply by 125,
you consult the decimal factor table and locate that
number beside the fraction 1/8. You tack three 0's onto
the other multiplier, because 125 contains three digits,
and multiply by 1/8 — which is the same as dividing by
8. Like this:

$$3\,2\,8 \times 1\,2\,5 = \frac{3\,2\,8,0\,0\,0}{8} = 4\,1,0\,0\,0$$

But to divide by 125, you reverse that process.

1. You consult the decimal factor table (you should
know it from memory, by the way) and locate that
fraction, 1/8.

2. You remove three 0's, if they're available, or else
move the decimal point three places to the left, because
125 contains three digits. (Adding three 0's for the
process of multiplication, in effect, moved the decimal
point three places to the right.)

3. You turn the fraction upside down, and multiply
it and the adjusted dividend. For example:

$$1\,2\,5\,\overline{/\,8\,3\,7\,5} = 8.3\,7\,5 \times \frac{8}{1} = 6\,7$$

(Multiply 8.375 × 8 — see for yourself!)

So the procedure for dividing with the use of the
easy-division device can be formulated as follows:

1. Move the dividend's decimal point as many places
to the left as there are digits in the divisor.

2. Turn the divisor's fraction-equivalent upside down, and multiply.

Here's another example of the easy-division device at work:

If you paid $100 for a gross (144) of golf balls, how much would you be blowing every time you sliced one into a pond?

THE PROBLEM: 1 4 4 $\overline{\smash{)}\$1 0 0.0 0}$

STEP ONE: Move the dividend's decimal point three places to the left, since the divisor contains three digits. This makes the dividend .10 — 10¢.

STEP TWO: Find the divisor's fraction equivalent in the decimal-factor table; invert it, and multiply. The closest number to 144 in the table is 143; its fraction equivalent to 1/7. Turn it upside down — 7/1 — and multiply.
.10 × 7 = .70.

Therefore, each golf ball costs approximately 70¢.

When the fraction equivalent of the divisor contains a numerator other than 1 (such as 3/4), you simply:

1. Invert the fraction as usual (make it 4/3)

2. Multiply by the new numerator (4)

3. Then divide by the new denominator (3). Watch:

$$625\overline{)23,750}$$

The fractional equivalent of 625 is 5/8, so I move the decimal point of the dividend three places to the left, and multiply by 8/5:

$$
\begin{array}{r}
2\,3\,.\,7\,5 \\
\times\ 8 \\
\hline
1\,6\,4\quad 6\,0 \\
2\,5\quad 4 \\
\hline
5\,\overline{)\,1\,9\,0\,.\,0\,0} \\
3\,8\,.
\end{array}
$$

Now you try it. Use the easy-division device to solve the long division problems in this

DRILL IN DIVIDING WITH THE
EASY-DIVISION DEVICE

[1.] $25\overline{)1,200}$ [2.] $375\overline{)3,375}$

[3.] $125\overline{)2,125}$ [4.] $625\overline{)19,375}$

[5.] $875\overline{)36,750}$ [6.] $250\overline{)79,750}$

[7.] $375\overline{)49,500}$ [8.] $750\overline{)10,500}$

[9.] $1,250\overline{)11,250}$ [10.] $625\overline{)266,250}$

SIMPLIFYING LONG DIVISION WITH
THE TEMPORARY DOUBLE

Once again, in order to be able to apply this short-cut device to long division we've got to make some adjustments in the method by which it was used to simplify multiplication.

You remember from Chapter 6 that we can double a multiplier in order to turn it into an easier-to-handle number — as long as we either cut the problem's product in half, or cut the other multiplier in half before multiplying.

(Besides doubling-and-halving, of course, we can triple-and-third, quadruple-and-quarter, or multiply-and-divide simultaneously by any number which simplifies one or both of the multipliers.)

So, as we've seen in multiplication, doubling a multiplier results in a double-size product; therefore it's necessary to cut the product in half. But watch what happens when we double the divisor in a division problem:

$$3\overline{)\,5\,4\,}^{1\,8} \qquad\qquad 6\overline{)\,5\,4\,}^{9}$$

Doubling the divisor resulted not in a double-size quotient, but in a half-size quotient.

So in order to compensate for the temporary double of a divisor, it's necessary to double the quotient also. Or double the dividend, before dividing.

To demonstrate, let me show you how the temporary double device is used to simplify the work required to solve the problem of 810 ÷ 45:

$$45\overline{)\,8\,1\,0\,} \;=\; 90\overline{)\,8\,1\,0\,}^{9\,\times\,2\,=\,1\,8} \qquad\qquad \underline{\text{or}}$$

$$90\overline{)\,1\,6\,2\,0\,}^{1\,8}$$

In the first solution I doubled the divisor, then divided (9 goes into 81 nine times), and then doubled the quotient to compensate for having doubled the divisor.

In the second solution I doubled both the divisor and the dividend so that compensation was made immediately, and performed the simple short division calculation of $162 \div 9$.

There's an added feature in the application of the temporary double device for simplifying division: besides doubling-and-doubling, it's possible, and often quite desirable, to halve-and-halve. Or third-and-third:

$$27\overline{)4,617} \quad \text{(quotient } 171)$$

Since the digit sums of both divisor and dividend are divisible by three, this problem can be adjusted to read

$$9\overline{)1539} \quad \text{(quotient } 171)$$

without changing the value of the quotient. The advantages of this alternative are quite apparent, don't you agree? As a matter of fact, it's good policy, when you can conveniently get away with it, to cut in half divisor and dividend of any division problem in which both end in even numbers.

$$192\overline{)2,688} = 96\overline{)1,344} = 48\overline{)672} =$$

$$24\overline{)336} = 12\overline{)168} = 6\overline{)84} \quad \text{(quotient } 14)$$

Now it's your turn. Use the temporary double (or triple, or sextuple, or quarter, or seventh, etc.) device to solve the problems in this

DRILL IN DIVIDING WITH THE
TEMPORARY DOUBLE DEVICE

[1.] 45/1,215   [2.] 35/3,115

[3.] 18/42,804   [4.] 27/1,728

[5.] 14/812   [6.] 16/68,384

[7.] 15/1,065   [8.] 21/1,113

[9.] 14/45,836   [10.] 45/4,410

And with all that under your belt, put your compre-
hensive thinking cap on, decide which short-cut device
or devices, if any, you'll use to solve each of the following long division problems, and take your

FINAL EXAM IN LONG DIVISION
WITH MODERN METHODS

1. $42\overline{)16,338}$ **2.** $144\overline{)7,056}$

3. $729\overline{)24,786}$ **4.** $99\overline{)33,759}$

5. $35\overline{)31,395}$ **6.** $36\overline{)17,244}$

7. $375\overline{)35,250}$ **8.** $29\overline{)58,087}$

9. $417\overline{)62,479}$ **10.** $89\overline{)428,002}$

CHAPTER NINE

Instant Proof: How To
Check Your Figures
Instantaneously And Never
Be In Doubt Of Your Work

This chapter alone can slash your work time in
half! Until this moment, if you wanted to be
sure your work was right, you had to solve every
problem TWICE — once to find the answer; and
then once again, backward, just to make sure
your answer was right. Now, you need only run
your eyes across the figures you've written, and
— because of a startling fact about our numerical
system — SEE AT A GLANCE that your work
is perfect.

"Prove all things, . . ."
— I Thessalonians, V: 21

I'm going to show you a simple little trick which you
can learn in minutes — and which will save nearly <u>half</u>
<u>the time you spend on mathematical calculation</u>!

You are probably the kind of person to whom being right means a lot. I'll bet that you always carefully fill in your checkbook stubs . . . never think of sending in your income tax return until you've checked and rechecked your figures . . . always make sure you haven't miscalculated before you start to spend money, at business or in the household budget.

You must be that kind of person, because if you weren't concerned about being accurate with figures, you wouldn't have your nose in this book right now. If you weren't vitally concerned about being able to get correct answers every time, you wouldn't be here looking for the best ways to put numbers together and take them apart.

So you're the kind of person who'd like to prove the answer to every mathematical problem you solve! You're simply not satisfied with your calculations until you've checked them out and assured their accuracy.

But if you've been running your checks the way they taught you at school, then you're spending practically as much time checking answers as you are solving problems.

For example, to check your answers in addition problems, you've been adding columns in the opposite direction as a check — adding up the columns instead of down:

Solution	Check
3	3 — 3 6
·8	·8
4	4
·7	·7
5	·5
·9	9
3 6	

To check your answers in subtraction, you've been adding your answer to the number which was subtracted, to see if the sum equaled the larger number:

Solution	Check
4 8,8 4 7	2 7,6 3 4
− 2 7,6 3 4	+ 2 1,2 1 3
2 1,2 1 3	4 8,8 4 7

To check your answers in multiplication, you've been dividing your answer by one of the multipliers, to see if the quotient was the other multiplier:

Solution

```
    4 5
  × 3 9
  1 2 5 5
  1 6
  3 4
1 6 5 5  =  1,755
```

Check

```
3 9 / 1 7 5 5 | 4 0
      1 5 6 0 |
        1 9 5 | 5
        1 9 5 |
          0   | 4 5
```

And to check problems in division, you've been multiplying your answer by the divisor, to see if the product was the dividend:

| Solution | Check |
| | |

```
        Solution                    Check

    1 7 / 8 1 6 | 4 0                 4 8
        6 8 0 |                      × 1 7
        _____|                      _____
        ₂3 6 | 8                      4 8 6
        1 3 6 |                       2 8
        _____|                      _____
            0 | 4 8                      5
                                      _____
                                      8 1 6
```

And if your division solution had had a remainder, you'd have added that remainder to the product of your check-multiplication.

A MIRACLE DEVICE TO ELIMINATE LENGTHY CHECKS

But now all that is in your past; you'll never again have to work out another entire mathematical problem in order to be sure that your original answer is correct.

You were doing every problem twice — but from now on, you'll simply look at the problem you've already solved, and see at a glance the proof that it's correct.

The remarkable time-saver that makes this possible is a simple device that the "pros" have been using for years. These men who earn their livelihoods by working with numbers — accountants, engineers, scientists — can't afford to waste their time solving every problem twice. So they prove their work — by adding digit sums to find the digital root!

That's what I said — they add digit sums to find the digital root. This lightning-quick device proves their work correct, or incorrect — in an instant.

And this incredibly simple device — which works its magic as effectively in addition, subtraction, multiplication and division — is as easy for YOU to use as this:

WHAT IS A DIGITAL ROOT?

The digital root of any number is: the sum of the number's digits added continuously until only one digit remains. The digital root of 36 is 9, because 3 + 6 = 9. The digital root of 134 is 1 + 3 + 4 = 8.   And the digital root of 26 is 2 + 6, or also 8.

The digital root of any number is found by adding together the digits of the number, and then re-adding the digits, if their sum equals more than 9.

For example, the digital root of 34 = 3 + 4 = 7. But the digital root of 385 is also 7; because 3 + 8 + 5 = 16, and then 1 + 6 = 7. (Remember we are adding and re-adding until our answer becomes a single digit.)

The digital root of 888,888 is 3, because six 8's are 48; then 4 + 8 = 12; and 1 + 2 = 3. (Again, our answer must be a single digit. No more.)

The digital root of 59 is 5. Because 5 + 9 = 14; and then 1 + 4 = 5. The digital root of 437 is 5. Do you know why? And what's the digital root of 77?

Here. Do some more.

DRILL NO. 1 ON FIGURING DIGITAL ROOTS

What are the digital roots of each of the following numbers?

1.	23	2.	32	3.	311	4.	131
5.	113	6.	320	7.	3,101	8.	42
9.	87	10.	168	11.	109	12.	823
13.	487	14.	703	15.	86	16.	898
17.	625	18.	4,382	19.	1,004	20.	7,853

HOW TO USE DIGITAL ROOTS TO MAKE
SURE YOU'RE RIGHT IN ADDITION

But how do digital roots <u>prove</u> the answers to problems you've solved are correct? Well, it's a funny thing, but:

<u>When two — or more — numbers are added correctly, their digital roots will equal the digital root of the answer.</u> Like this:

1. Add the problem:

    3 8 4

    4 6 4

    2 3 6

    9 7 4 = 1,084

2. Find the digital root of the answer:

    1 + 0 + 8 + 4 = 13;   1 + 3 = 4

3. Add up the digital roots of each number in the problem:

    3 + 8 + 4 = 15;   1 + 5 =   6

    4 + 6 + 4 = 14;   1 + 4 =   5

    2 + 3 + 6 = 11;   1 + 1 =   2

                        1 3 − 1 + 3 = 4

The digital roots of those three numbers — 6, 5, and 2 — add up to 13, which reduces to a root of 4. The digital root of the answer is 4 also, <u>so the answer is correct.</u> It's as simple as that!

HOW TO USE DIGITAL ROOTS TO MAKE SURE YOU'RE RIGHT IN SUBTRACTION

In exactly the same way, when a number is <u>sub-tracted</u> from another number, the digital roots of the <u>bottom</u> number and the <u>answer</u> will add up to the digital root of the <u>top</u> number. Like this:

1. Subtract the problem:

$$
\begin{array}{r}
6,5\ 7\ 8 \\
-\ 4,3\ 1\ 3 \\
\hline
2,2\ 6\ 5
\end{array}
$$

2. Find the digital roots of both numbers and the answer:

$$6 + 5 + 7 + 8 = 26; \quad 2 + 6 = 8$$

$$4 + 3 + 1 + 3 = 11; \quad 1 + 1 = 2$$

$$2 + 2 + 6 + 5 = 15; \quad 1 + 5 = 6$$

3. Add the two bottom roots. They should equal the top one.

$$6 + 2 = 8$$

Do you see? The digital root of the bottom number plus the digital root of the answer equals the digital root of the top number; therefore, the answer is correct.

HOW TO USE DIGITAL ROOTS TO MAKE SURE YOU'RE RIGHT IN MULTIPLICATION

When two numbers are multiplied correctly, the product of their digital roots will of course equal the digital root of the answer. Like this:

1. Multiply the problem:

$$
\begin{array}{r}
1\ 0\ 1 \\
\times\ 3\ 4 \\
\hline
3,4\ 3\ 4
\end{array}
$$

2. Find the digital roots:

$$1 + 0 + 1\ =\ 2$$

$$3 + 4\ =\ 7$$

$$3 + 4 + 3 + 4\ =\ 14;\ 1 + 4\ =\ 5$$

3. Multiply the digital roots of the two numbers. They should equal the digital root of the answer. (Remember: always reduce the digit sum to a single digit.)

See how simple it is? When the digital roots of this problem's multipliers are themselves multiplied, they produce a final digital root of 5. And since that's the digital root of the problem's answer, that answer is correct.

HOW TO USE DIGITAL ROOTS TO MAKE SURE YOU'RE RIGHT IN DIVISION

When one number is divided by another, the product of the divisor's digital root and the answer's digital root will equal the digital root of the dividend.

1. Divide the problem:

$$
\begin{array}{r}
8\,9 \\[-2pt]
4\,\overline{/\,3\,5\,6} \\[-2pt]
3\,2\,\overline{/\,2{,}8\,4\,8} \quad - \quad 8\,\overline{/\,2\,8\,4\,8}
\end{array}
$$

2. To check, multiply the digital roots of the divisor and the answer. They should equal the digital root of the dividend.

Dividend: $2 + 8 + 4 + 8 = 22;$ $2 + 2 = 4$

Divisor: $3 + 2 = 5$

Answer: $8 + 9 = 17;$ $1 + 7 = 8$
          $5 \times 8 = 40;$ $4 + 0 = 4.$

The product of the divisor's digital root (5) and the digital root of the answer (8) is $40 = 4 + 0 = 4$. And since that's the digital root of the dividend, the answer to the problem is correct.

Now what about remainders? In the event that your division problem doesn't work out evenly — in the event that after dividing you're left with a remainder — then you simply add the remainder's digital root to the product of the digital roots of the answer and the divisor. Like this:

1. This is the problem:

```
4 3 / 7 8 6 | 1 0
      4 3 0 |
      3 5 6 | 7
      3 0 1 |
        5 5 | 1
        4 3 |
        1 2 | 1 8, remainder 1 2
```

2. Multiply the digital roots of the divisor and the answer:

Divisor: $4 + 3 = 7$

Answer: $1 + 8 = 9$

$7 \times 9 = 63$; $6 + 3 = 9$

3. Add the digital root of the remainder to the product of the digital roots of the divisor and the answer. This should equal the digital root of the dividend.

The remainder is 12, the digital root of which is — 3. Add this to 9, the product of the divisor and answer digital roots.

$9 + 3 = 12$; $1 + 2 = 3$

Dividend: $7 + 8 + 6 = 21$; $2 + 1 = 3$

Again it works out right. The product of the digital roots of the divisor (7) and the answer (9) is 63. $6 + 3 = 9$. Add the digital root of the remainder (3) to that, and the final digital root is $9 + 3 = 12$; $1 + 2 = 3$. Since that's the digital root of the problem's dividend, the answer is correct.

THERE IT IS — AS SIMPLE AS THAT!

So the digital roots of the numbers in any kind of mathematics problem can be used to check the accuracy of the problem's answer. You don't have to solve the problem all over again; you don't have to work out a whole new calculation in another process to prove the correctness of your answer.

Instead, from now on, simply see the relationships between the numbers' digital roots, and determine from your knowledge of the addition and multiplication tables whether the answer is correct. (You're actually proving as you've always done, except you're working with easy-to-handle digital roots instead of the cumbersome large numbers.)

Try some for yourself. Add, subtract, multiply, or divide to solve the problems in this first drill in using the digital roots, and then use the digital root to prove that you found the right answers. If you've done it right, you'll find the following to be true:

Addition: The sum of the digital roots equals the digital root of the answer.

Subtraction: The sum of the digital roots of the answer and the bottom number equals the digital root of the top number.

Multiplication: The product of the multiplier's digital roots equals the digital root of the answer.

Division: The product of the digital roots of the divisor and the answer — plus the digital root of the remainder, if any — equals the digital root of the dividend.

Do them right, now. See how easy it is!

DRILL NO. 1 IN CHECKING
WITH DIGITAL ROOTS

ADDITION

1.	4 1 8	2.	3 4 2	3.	9 4 3
	9 2 3		9 1 8		1 5 0
	7 6 4		4 5 4		8 7 2

SUBTRACTION

4.	4,5 2 7	5.	7,2 4 3	6.	4,9 6 4
	− 3 8 8		− 3,8 1 1		− 2,7 2 7

MULTIPLICATION

7.	5 6	8.	7 9	9.	9 7
	× 3 7		× 5 8		× 8 5

DIVISION

10. 26 / 3 3 8

11. 4 7 / 1,8 4 9

12. 3 9 / 4,2 2 7

HOW DIGITAL ROOTS SHOW YOU
WHERE YOU WENT WRONG

Wonderful! From now on, you can verify the accuracy of your calculations by manipulating digital roots. You no longer have to do every problem twice. You eliminate the possibility of repeating an error and failing to notice it because the answers in the problem and the check-problem are identical. And you never have to work out the solution for a problem a third time, because you're not sure which of two conflicting answers — if either — is correct.

By using digital roots to check your work you don't do the work over. And if the answer's wrong, you'll have a good idea of how wrong it is, by noting how far off the digital root is. Like this:

The Problem	Digital Roots
4 7	2
·8 ·5	4
5 6	2
·3 ·5	8
3 3	6
2 3 4	2 2 = 4
2 5 4 = 11 = 2	

The answer's digital root — 2 — is 2 too small. That means that probably one of the digits in the answer is 2 too small. A useful clue, when you go back to find out where you went wrong. (Check the problem and see.)

BUT WAIT! LET'S SAVE EVEN MORE TIME!

As I say, it's wonderful. But where's the wonderful saving in time and work, when it takes you nearly as long to figure out all those digital roots as it would to work out the problem a second time? The answer to that question lies in a simple refinement that makes finding digital roots instantaneous! It's called:

CASTING OUT NINES

You might have noticed an interesting "phenomenon" regarding digital roots, while you studied these pages and checked the problems in the drill; that the addition of a 9 to any digital root did nothing to change it!

Thus, the digital root of 49 is 13, which is 4. The digital root of 92 is 11, which is 2. The digital root of 9,959,999 is 5. Figure it out, and prove it to yourself. (You just eliminate 9's — no need to do any adding here.)

Now, what are the digital roots of these numbers:

        2,2 2 9 =
        2,9 9 1 =
        9 9 9 =
        9,9 9 9,9 9 9,9 9 9,9 9 5 =

Answers:

        6
        3
        9 (or 0)
        5

Now why do you suppose that that's so? It's because 9 = 10 − 1.   And the digital roots of both 10 and 1 are 1. And, therefore, every time you add 9 to a number you are, in effect, <u>adding 1 to its digital root and subtracting 1 from its digital root.</u> So you don't change it at all! (Look at it this way: to find the digital root of <u>any</u> number, you are <u>casting out</u> (or dropping) all the 9's from that number.)

Does it work with two numbers that <u>equal</u> 9? What's the digital root of 163? Of 459? Of 45,459,729? It <u>does</u> work, and the fact that it does makes all the difference in the world!

I'm sure you've already realized that you can ignore 0's when calculating digital roots — the digital root of 80 is 8, and the digital root of 800,000,000,000, is 8.

<u>Now I'm telling you that you can ignore 9's as well!</u> Every time you come across a pair of numbers that <u>equal</u> 9, you can toss them out too!

Now watch how easy this new discovery makes it to calculate a digital root:

$$4\ 0\ 9,6\ 3\ 2,9\ 0\ 1$$

Remember the 4: then cross out the zero and the 9. Then add the 6 and the 3 to get 9, and cross them out too. Now add the 2 to the 4 to get 6. Cross out the next 0 and the 9. And then add the final 1 to your 6 to get the digital root of 7. <u>Here's what the same problem looks like after you've dropped the nines:</u>

$$4\ \cancel{0}\ \cancel{9},\ \cancel{0}\ \cancel{3}\ 2,\ \cancel{9}\ \cancel{0}\ 1 = 4 + 2 + 1 = 7$$

If you had done it the old way — by adding <u>all</u> the numbers, you would have found that the digits in the number total 34, and the digital root is therefore 7, <u>but by skipping over 9's, 0's, and numbers that add up to 9, you will arrive at precisely the same answer — in seconds!</u>

Try doing the same thing with these numbers.

DRILL NO. 2 IN FIGURING
DIGITAL ROOTS — FASTER

What are the digital roots of these numbers?

1.	1 9	2.	2 9
3.	2 9 9	4.	2 9,9 7 2
5.	4 5,3 6 9	6.	3 8 4
7.	4,8 1 3	8.	8 1,8 1 4
9.	3,9 6 4	10.	7,5 4 9
11.	5 3,2 9 4	12.	4 3 2,4 3 2,4 3 2
13.	4,7 2 8	14.	1 7,4 8 7
15.	8 4 6,3 5 1,7 2 9	16.	4 7 9,0 0 8,5 2 1
17.	3 2 5	18.	3 2 6
19.	3 2 7	20.	4,0 0 0,0 0 0

CASTING OUT 9's FOR LIGHTNING-
QUICK CHECKING

Now that figuring digital roots is barely harder —
and takes you hardly longer — than reading numbers,
you'll enjoy reviewing the subject of using digital roots
to check answers in actual problems.

So let's take another look at each of those procedures
for checking answers, paying special attention to the
manner in which casting out 9's speeds the procedure.

CASTING OUT 9's TO SPEED-
CHECK ADDITION

Again, the sum of the digital roots should be equal to
the digital root of the answer. But now you do it this
way:

```
  6 3 8  —  Ignore the 6 and 3 =   8

 ·9 1 ·4  —  Ignore the 9        =   5

 ·7 2 ·8  —  Ignore the 7 and 2 =   8

  2 3 4  —  Ignore everything!

  3 ·4 5  —  Ignore the 4 and 5 =    3

2 7 3 9                            2 4  =  6

2,8 5 9  —  Ignore the 9 = 15  = 6
```

In the first number, two of the digits equal 9; like-
wise in the third and fifth numbers in the problem.
Therefore, the digital roots of each of those numbers
was the remaining digit.

There's a 9 in that second number, so the digital root
is simply the sum of the other two digits.

And in the fourth number, all three digits total 9 and can be completely ignored.

And at the same time, the answer contains a 9, which is ignored when its digital root is figured.

CASTING OUT 9's TO SPEED-CHECK SUBTRACTION

The digital root of the bottom number and the digital root of the answer, when combined, should equal the digital root of the top number:

$$48,621 - \text{Ignore the last three digits} = 3$$

$$-\underline{23,540} - \text{Ignore the last three digits} = 5$$

$$25,\not{1}81$$

$$25,081 - \text{Ignore the last three digits} = 7$$

$$7 + 5 = 12; \quad 1 + 2 = 3$$

CASTING OUT 9's TO SPEED-CHECK MULTIPLICATION

The product of the multipliers' digital roots should equal the digital root of the answer:

$$9 \ 8 - \text{Ignore the 9} = \quad 8$$

$$\underline{\times 3 \ 9} - \text{Ignore the 9} = \underline{\times 3}$$

$$2 \ 7 \ 4 \ 2 \qquad\qquad\qquad 2 \ 4 = 6$$

$$2 \ 1$$

$$\underline{8 \ 7}$$

$$\underline{2} \ \underline{7} \ 2 \ 2 = 3,822 = 15 = 6$$

And one more multiplication problem:

```
      9 4 5  —  Ignore everything! The digital
      ×  8 7     root is 0
  ─────────
  7 2 2 0 5
      3 4 8
      6 3 3
      2
  ─────────
  7̲ 1̲ 1̲ 1 5  =  8 2 , 2 1 5  =  9, which is the
                              same as 0
```

After a bit of practice, you'll be able to look at a number like 82215 and know almost instantly that the digital root is zero. Because you will see the 8 and 1, which add to 9, and cancels out. Remaining are a 2, 2 and 5, which also total 9 and are dropped.

9 is the same as 0 because you're casting out all 9's. Take away 9 from 9 and you're left with 0.

And in this last problem, it isn't even necessary to compute the digital root of the second multiplier — since you are going to multiply it by the digital root of the first multiplier, which is 0, and anything multiplied by 0 always equals 0.

And since the answer's digital root is also 0, the solution is correct.

CASTING OUT 9's TO SPEED-CHECK DIVISION

The digital root of the dividend should equal the product of the digital roots of the divisor and the answer plus the digital root of the remainder, if any:

```
49/54,836      1000      Dividend: Ignore first two
   49 000                           and last two
   ̶ ̶ ̶ ̶ ̶ ̶                           digits — 8
    5 836       100
    4 900                 Divisor:  Ignore 9 —   4
   ̶ ̶ ̶ ̶ ̶ ̶                                     ×
      936        10      Answer:   Ignore 9 —   3
      490                                      ̶ ̶
   ̶ ̶ ̶ ̶ ̶ ̶                                      1 2
      546         8                             +
      392                Remainder:             5
   ̶ ̶ ̶ ̶ ̶ ̶                                     ̶ ̶ ̶
      154         1                             1 7 — 8
       49
   ̶ ̶ ̶ ̶ ̶ ̶
        5      1119
```

Of all the digits in the dividend, only the center one
was used, since the others canceled each other out.
Both the divisor and the answer contained 9's that were
canceled.

ONE SMALL CAUTION

By now you should know exactly what's what in this
remarkable business of casting out 9's. You should
understand the rules for checking answers in all four
mathematical processes with digital roots. You should
know every time-saving trick in figuring digital roots,
from skipping 0's to combining 5's and 4's, 7's and 2's,
6's and 3's, 8's and 1's to make 9's, and then dropping
them.

And you should be supremely confident, by now, that
this unusual device for proving accuracy really works.

Now, stop right here for just a minute, and pay attention while I let you in on the only loophole in the
game of casting out 9's.

If while solving a problem you should happen to make two mistakes — one of which made one of the digits in the answer higher by 1 while the other mistake made another answer-digit lower by 1 — then the digital root wouldn't reveal that dual boo-boo, would it? And if you should happen to make a mistake by 9 — casting out 9's wouldn't reveal that, either.

Thank goodness that your new excellence in using the modern methods of adding, subtracting, multiplying and dividing makes the odds a thousand to one against your ever making either two such mistakes or a mistake by 9 in any problem!

But even if such an impossible-seeming occurrence should come to pass, I'd be willing to bet that when you were reading that problem over, when you were scanning those figures to compute digital roots and check the answer, there'd be something about the whole problem that would sit funny with you.

You see, after all the time that you've spent at work with this book, you're sure to have sharpened your number sense to a point where it's almost an extra sense. So let's not worry too much about that rare occurrence!

Now our last practice. As quickly as you can, figure the digital roots of the numbers on page 220.

FINAL DRILL IN FIGURING DIGITAL
ROOTS — THE FASTEST WAY

Use all the short cuts to determine the digital roots of these numbers.

1.	472,936,458,120
2.	111,111,111,422
3.	890,126,473,889
4.	423,725,084,221
5.	716,447,888,204
6.	828,738,666,417
7.	572,643,829,400
8.	493,828,476,532
9.	408,809,724,622
10.	824,647,338,114
11.	847,008,329,145
12.	428,824,428,824
13.	396,814,472,604
14.	827,814,483,467
15.	367,781,004,328
16.	818,964,631,007
17.	721,083,345,678
18.	123,456,654,038

[19.]   3 2 7,7 1 4,5 3 9,6 1 1

[20.]   6 1 6,4 7 2,8 8 9,9 8 4

YOUR FINAL EXAM IN SOLVING —
AND PROVING — PROBLEMS IN
ADDITION, SUBTRACTION,
MULTIPLICATION AND DIVISION

With that behind you, here are 50 mathematics
problems — you'll never have to solve any problems
that will be harder than these — to test every technique,
every short cut, every device that you've learned within
these pages. Do your best, now, and calculate 50 correct answers. Because when you're finished you've got
to prove 50 answers with the casting out 9's technique!

FINAL EXAM IN ALL PROCEDURES
OF MODERN MATHEMATICS

1.   8 9
     6 4
     3 3
     2 4
     7 7
     2 8
     6 4
     8 8
     7 9
     1 1

2.   3 9, 6 4 7
  − 8, 7 5 7

3.   4 8
   × 2 9

4.   3 3
  × 2 1

5.   7 8 4
   9 2 7
   6 4 3
   3 7 8
   4 1 9

6.   4 8 6
   3 2 9
   7 1 8
   8 2 7
   6 4 3

7. 48,723
   − 26,488

8. 37 / 592

9. 37
   × 2 3

10. 1 1
    1 8
    2 3
    4 4
    7 6
    3 7
    8 8
    2 4
    1 6
    7 7

11. 3 4 2, 4 2 1
    − 8 7, 6 4 9

12. 8 7
    × 7 4

13.   3 3 4 , 0 9 3
        -   3 4 , 2 0 7

14.   8 4 6
        3 8 8
        4 1 7
        9 9 6
        4 3 3

15.   6 4
        × 4 8

16.   6 8 8
        ×   3 7

17.   4 3 / 3 0 1

18.   5 6 / 4 , 9 8 4

19.   4 9
        × 7 4

20.   3 8 9
        ×   7 6

21.

```
2 8
4 8
5 8
3 8
6 8
4 3
2 3
4 3
7 3
8 3
```

22. $28\overline{)1,372}$

23.

```
  1 8 , 4 2 9
-     9 , 9 9 9
```

24.

```
  4 2 7 , 8 9 3
-   3 7 , 9 8 4
```

25.

```
  4 , 8 7 2
+ 3 , 8 4 4
```

26. $324\overline{)2,592}$

27.   8 3 1   28.   4 7
       7 9 1   8 9
       4 0 3   6 4
       9 8 4   3 3
       6 8 6   2 8
                             7 7
                             1 4
                             1 6
                             2 8
                             3 4

29.   4 9 , 6 2 3   30.   9 8 8
     + 1 7 , 8 1 9   × 9 3 7

31.   4 1 8   32.   4 1 9 / 1 3 , 8 2 7
       ×   3 7

33. $87 \overline{)6,003}$

34. 474
    × 38

35.   596
    × 74

36. $489 \overline{)353,547}$

37. $13 \overline{)615}$

38.   84
    × 37

39.   437,624
    − 88,737

40.   846
    × 329

41. $43 \overline{)3,752}$

42. $26 \overline{)1,120}$

43.   4 7 4   44.   3 4 , 7 8 4
      ×   8 9   + 1 6 , 8 2 9

45.   3 8 9   46.   4 7 , 8 1 9
      ×   4 7   + 2 8 , 4 7 2

47.   7 8 / 2 7 , 2 4 5   48.   4 9 / 5 4 3

49.   2 6 4 / 2 2 , 9 8 5   50.   2 8 7 / 1 0 4 , 4 7 2

Postscript

"There aren't any rules for success
that work unless you do!"

— "The Farmers' Almanac"

If you've read these pages and followed my instructions carefully, if you've studied all the techniques and answered all the quizzes and worked out all the drills, then I don't have to say anything more to you . . . You know how effective these devices and techniques really are. And you don't have to be told where and when to put them to work, because they've become a living part of your basic thinking.

I hope you realize that I couldn't possibly mention and describe every single detail — every combination of devices — since it would have taken a book at least twice this size. But if you understand and use the ideas and techniques, you'll eventually be creating short cuts of the short cuts!

But if you've given the book no more than a hasty reading, stopping every now and again to "test" the things I've told you, then I feel that I owe you the words that follow . . . because if you haven't mastered math, you haven't gotten your money's worth.

So now I must persuade you to give yourself a real
chance to master the modern methods that I've described in this book. I've got to give you some sort of
demonstration of their practical application . . . in your
life.

Do you own a car? I know a man who figured out —
mentally — how much it cost him to drive one mile
(including gasoline, garaging, depreciation, and so
forth), and discovered that he could save several
hundred dollars a year by renting a car.

Do you know the tricks of stretching your shopping
dollars? Can you quickly determine which brands
are the most economical, even when every manufacturer packages his product in a different size
container?

Are you a card player? You know that it's harder
to draw a fifth spade than a third trey, but do you
know how much harder? Do you play the odds, or
the blind hunches? There are 52 cards in the deck;
you can narrow the odds — actually turn them in
your favor — with every turn of a card, if you can
calculate mentally, quickly, and accurately.

Do you dabble in sewing . . . knitting . . . crochet-
ing . . . cooking . . . carpentry . . . modeling. . .
gardening? Mathematics can help you to save
dollars by conserving materials and equipment; it
can help you estimate the best ways to plan your
activities, so that you save time — and worry — all
around.

Do you work with figures? The more time you spend
with figures on your job, the more important a strong
understanding of modern mathematical techniques and
methods will be for you. If you can quickly dispatch

mathematical chores that keep your associates busy for hours on end, your superiors _must_ recognize your abilities.

No matter who you are, no matter what you do, you're going to need mathematics every day of your life. You'll need mathematics when you plan a budget, when you decide whether to buy a new bedroom suite, when you estimate how long it'll take to drive to your mother's place, when you watch a ball game, when you invite people to share a meal with you, when you paint the living room, when you put up bookshelves . . . .

Suppose, just for the sake of discussion, that you now have to spend even as little as ten minutes a day on calculating solutions to mathematical problems. That's still over an hour a week, every week of your life! This means that the equivalent of two and a half days out of every year you live will be spent adding, subtracting, multiplying, and dividing!

Now, I can promise you, with complete confidence, that after you've read this book the way I've asked you to read it, you can cut that time at least in half! That means that in the next twenty years, I'll have saved you over 600 work-hours! That's more than enough extra time to take your family on a wonderful vacation!

It's all simple mathematics! So why not go over the book just once more until you've mastered math, until you've built a true "mental computer" into your brain, until you're saving time, money, mistakes and needless effort every time you pick up your pencil to flash through any math problem — anywhere — that you're confronted with.

Remember — the better you are at math, the more money you earn! So don't stop till every one of these secrets is second nature to you!

Good figuring and good luck!

ANSWERS TO ALL MATHEMATICAL DRILLS

CHAPTER 1
HOW TO ADD FASTER THAN AN ADDING MACHINE

Page 14: Drill in Adding Without Carrying

1.	52	2.	62	3.	61	.4.	48
5.	54	6.	54	7.	51	8.	56
9.	50	10.	60	11.	71	12.	63
13.	49	14.	58	15.	70	16.	87
17.	74	18.	71	19.	58	20.	50

Page 23: Drill in Rapid Digit Combination

Reading across the columns, starting at upper left:

1.	·1	2.	9	3.	6	4.	·2	5.	7
6.	·6	7.	9	8.	·0	9.	·6	10.	·1
11.	·2	12.	·2	13.	·1	14.	·8	15.	·1
16.	·1	17.	·2	18.	·1	19.	·4	20.	·6
21.	7	22.	·2	23.	·0	24.	·2	25.	·2
26.	·8	27.	·5	28.	·3	29.	·0	30.	·2
31.	·1	32.	·5	33.	·8	34.	·2	35.	·1
36.	·1	37.	·1	38.	2	39.	·2	40.	·7
41.	·5	42.	·1	43.	·0	44.	·1	45.	·6
46.	·2	47.	·6	48.	·3	49.	·4	50.	8

Page 26: <u>Drill in Rapid Column Addition</u>

1.	50	2.	52	3.	51	4.	59
5.	61	6.	59	7.	63	8.	53
		9.	56	10.	54		

Page 37: <u>Drill in Left-to-Right Addition</u>

1.	15,796	2.	31,219	3.	15,508
4.	39,382	5.	61,105	6.	27,243
7.	35,099	8.	19,481	9.	49,211
10.	33,103	11.	44,153	12.	25,217
13.	31,619	14.	32,414	15.	30,151

Page 45: <u>Two-Column Addition</u>

1.	303	2.	332
3.	289	4.	363
5.	319	6.	315
7.	346	8.	360
9.	238	10.	230

Page 47: <u>Three-Column Addition</u>

1.	2,561	2.	2,511	3.	2,728	4.	3,715
5.	3,047	6.	2,825	7.	2,281	8.	3,976
		9.	3,681	10.	2,661		

Page 48: <u>Four-Column Addition</u>

1.	34511	2.	33997
3.	31369	4.	29184
5.	32112	6.	22077
7.	22662	8.	23460
9.	21292	10.	42055

Page 50: <u>Final Exam in Lightning Addition</u>

1.	36	2.	228
3.	2,456	4.	1,405,512.34
5.	626.79	6.	90
7.	1,012,000	8.	870
9.	499,254	10.	23,597
11.	9,144	12.	325.6056

CHAPTER 2

HOW TO SHIFT ADDITION INTO HIGH GEAR

Page 55: <u>Drill in Mental Addition — Finger Method</u>

1.	33	2.	39
3.	43	4.	40
5.	47	6.	35
7.	39	8.	49
9.	37	10.	33

Page 59: <u>Drill in Mental Addition (Estimating)—
Round-off Method</u>

(Your answers are only mental estimates of these exact
numbers.)

1.	533	2.	575
3.	590	4.	652
5.	570	6.	350
7.	505	8.	542
9.	658	10.	520

Page 62: <u>Drill in Mental Addition — Piece-Work Method</u>

1.	4,969		2.	99,388
3.	$ 44.73		4.	9,956
5.	112,983		6.	2,801
7.	$107.09		8.	161.12
9.	1,320		10.	$ 50.00

Page 65: <u>Drill in Mental Addition — Elevator Method</u>

1.	3,241		2.	2,796
3.	3,082		4.	3,375
5.	3,521		6.	2,742
7.	3,087		8.	2,438
9.	2,719		10.	12,884

Page 69: <u>Final Drill in Mental Addition</u>

1.	28,089		2.	51
3.	226		4.	2,840
5.	5,093		6.	$ 160.78
7.	50		8.	2,851
9.	414		10.	$246,847.35
11.	$481.95		12.	5,668

CHAPTER 3

HOW TO SUBTRACT WITHOUT BORROWING

Page 77: <u>Drill in Left-to-Right, Slash Method Subtraction</u>

1.	7	2.	8	3.	9	4.	29
5.	49	6.	4	7.	3	8.	19
9.	8	10.	19	11.	69	12.	49
13.	9	14.	38	15.	59	16.	29
17.	37	18.	27	19.	9	20.	59

Page 82: <u>Drill in Subtraction Possibilities</u>

1.	slash–5	2.	slash–9
3.	slash–6	4.	slash–6
5.	slash–4	6.	slash–7
7.	slash–8	8.	slash–8
9.	slash–9	10.	slash–7
11.	slash–9	12.	slash–9
13.	slash–8	14.	slash–9
15.	slash–9	16.	slash–8
17.	slash–8	18.	slash–9
19.	slash–3	20.	slash–4

Page 86:   Final Exam in Subtraction without Borrowing

1.	$ 197.10	2.	106 mi.
3.	$ 124.47	4.	87 games
5.	1.5 yds.	6.	880 yds.
7.	35 yrs.	8.	$ 112,376
9.	92,761,143 mi.	10.	$ 2.23
11.	$ 19.25	12.	93.75 ft. or 93' 9"

Page 90:   Drill in Subtracting with the Zeroing-In Device

1.	225	2.	485
3.	2,724	4.	456
5.	4,999	6.	904
7.	3,235	8.	6,898
9.	2,828	10.	1,547

Page 92:   Final Drill in Mental Subtraction —
Zeroing-In and Piece Work

1.	36	2.	317
3.	306	4.	87
5.	1,442	6.	1,879
7.	2,877	8.	5,578
9.	18,889	10.	384,736

CHAPTER 4

HOW TO MULTIPLY WITHOUT MULTIPLYING

Page 104: <u>First Drill in Easy Multiplication</u>

1.	392	2.	371
3.	552	4.	704
5.	532	6.	3,024
7.	1,896	8.	2,146
9.	4,356	10.	3,596

Page 109: <u>Drill in Multiplying without Multiplying</u>

1.	234	2.	304	3.	1,222
4.	61,101	5.	147	6.	2,432
7.	586,764	8.	1,344	9.	2,296
10.	2,553	11.	6,391	12.	13,148

Page 110: <u>Drill in Underlined Digits</u>

Reading down the columns, left column first:

5	10	4	10	3
7	7	8	4	9
9	6	4	9	8
9	3	11	5	7

Page 116: Final Exam in Multiplying without Multiplying

1.	$ 56.35	2.	$ 167.32
3.	44 1/4 inches	4.	$ 9,275.00
5.	11,180 lbs.	6.	8,568 mi.
7.	$ 3,457.32	8.	77 1/2 yds.
9.	1,042,368 cal.	10.	19,396,160 lbs.

CHAPTER 5

HOW TO SOLVE "IMPOSSIBLE" MULTI-PLICATION PROBLEMS — IN YOUR HEAD

Page 126: Drill No. 1 in Mental Breakdown

1.	36,135	2.	885,265
3.	1,452,922,218	4.	644,380
5.	558,360	6.	4,558,437
7.	8,557,549	8.	649,003,780
9.	339,966	10.	694,278

Page 131: <u>Drill No. 2 in Mental Breakdown</u>

1.	100 − 4	2.	20 + 1/10
3.	40 + 1/10	4.	70 + 1
5.	80 − 1/10	6.	10 + 1
7.	80 − 1	8.	70 − 1/10
9.	60 + 1/10	10.	60 − 1/10
11.	50 − 1/10	12.	50 + 1
13.	50 + 1/10	14.	50 − 1
15.	20 − 1/10	16.	300 − 1/10
17.	200 − 1	18.	30 − 1/10
19.	70 − 1	20.	20 − 1

Page 132: <u>Continuation of Drill No. 2</u>

1.	49,248	2.	11,286
3.	22,572	4.	36,423
5.	36,936	6.	40,527
7.	32,319	8.	33,858
9.	27,702	10.	23,085
11.	26,163	12.	5,643
13.	28,215	14.	25,137
15.	9,234	16.	138,510
17.	102,087	18.	13,851
19.	35,397	20.	9,747

CHAPTER 6

MORE MULTIPLICATION SHORT CUTS!

Page 138: Drill No. 1 in Factor-the-Matter Multiplication

1.	864	2.	864	3.	864
4.	864	5.	864	6.	864
7.	864	8.	864	9.	864

Page 142: Drill No. 2 in Factor-the-Matter Multiplication

1.	5,184	2.	11,775
3.	30,645	4.	38,416
5.	51,849	6.	10,956
7.	26,622	8.	41,328
9.	39,312	10.	28,714

Page 143: Drill in Short-Cut Multiplication — Free Style

1.	1,215	2.	4,752
3.	4,655	4.	2,646
5.	2,088	6.	15,552
7.	33,534	8.	7,776
9.	10,752	10.	7,176

Page 148: Drill on the Easy-Division Table
          for Rapid Estimating

1.	1/4	2.	3/5	3.	7/8	4.	3/8
5.	5/6	6.	1/9	7.	4/5	8.	1/8
9.	1/4	10.	7/8	11.	4/9	12.	2/7
13.	5/7	14.	1/2	15.	1/7	16.	1/3
17.	6/7	18.	2/9	19.	1/9	20.	1/9

Page 150: Drill No. 1 in Multiplying by the
          Easy-Division Device

1.	94,000	2.	78,000
3.	120	4.	131,131
5.	704,718	6.	112,112
7.	617,176	8.	82,170
9.	11,140,848	10.	3,055,504

Page 152: Drill No. 2 in Multiplying by the
          Easy-Division Device

1.	148,000	2.	20,000
3.	861,000	4.	54,000
5.	7,080	6.	$1,244.00
7.	$900.00	8.	100
9.	660	10.	1,659,000

Page 155: <u>Drill in Converting Multipliers for</u>
<u>the Easy-Division Device</u>

1.	125 − 1	2.	250 + 1/10	3.	375 − 10
4.	375 + 10	5.	8 × 2	6.	125 + 50
7.	500 − 5	8.	875 × 3	9.	875 × 2
10.	50 + 1/10	11.	625 − 2	12.	625 × 3

Page 158: <u>Drill No. 1 in Multiplying with the</u>
<u>Temporary Double Device</u>

1.	630	2.	1,080
3.	1,980	4.	1,200
5.	6,000	6.	3,960
7.	35,420	8.	27,540
9.	8,680	10.	21,550

Page 159: <u>Drill No. 2 in Multiplying with the</u>
<u>Temporary Double Device</u>

1.	1,600	2.	360
3.	189	4.	108
5.	16,650	6.	6,540
7.	2,550	8.	23,700
9.	3,000	10.	1,200

Page 162: Final Exam in Multiplication with
Short-Cut Devices

1.	3,168	2.	22,152
3.	5,500	4.	3,180
5.	3,762	6.	367.5
7.	13,700	8.	6,480
9.	12,048	10.	4,480

CHAPTER 7

HOW TO DIVIDE WITHOUT DIVIDING

Page 171: Drill in Long Division the Progressive
Subtraction Way

1.	43	2.	39
3.	221	4.	83
5.	12	6.	374
7.	421	8.	23
9.	295	10.	15 (remainder: 12)

Page 175: <u>Drill No. 1 in Estimating Quotients</u>

1. 50	**2.**	7	
3. 50	**4.**	300	
5. 200	**6.**	3 (You can see this one)	
7. 300	**8.**	5	
9. 100	**10.**	2,000,000	

Page 177: <u>Drill No. 2 in Estimating Quotients</u>

1. 4	**2.** 40	**3.** 500	**4.** 50	**5.** 5
6. 600	**7.** 2	**8.** 50	**9.** 1,000	**10.** 5

Page 181: <u>Your Final Exam in Progressive-Subtraction Division</u>

1. 74

2. 9

3. 64

4. 388

5. 239 (remainder: 210)

6. 3 (remainder: 4)

7. 399

8. 6 (remainder: 17)

9. 202 (remainder: 4)

10. 3,713,731 (remainder: 87)

CHAPTER 8

SHORT- CUT DEVICES FOR INCREASING
SPEED IN DIVISION

Page 188: <u>Drill in Dividing with Mental Breakdown</u>

1.	41	2.	302

3.	7,106	4.	5,001 (remainder: 3)

5. 30,104

Page 191: <u>Drill in Dividing with the
Factor-the-Matter Device</u>

1.	22	2.	318
3.	437	4.	19
5.	34	6.	876
7.	1,247	8.	37
9.	14	10.	7,002

Page 194: <u>Drill in Dividing with the Easy-Division Device</u>

1.	48	2.	9
3.	17	4.	31
5.	42	6.	319
7.	132	8.	14
9.	9	10.	426

Page 197: <u>Drill in Dividing with the Temporary</u>
<u>Double Device</u>

[1.] 27   [2.] 89   [3.] 2,378

[4.] 64   [5.] 58   [6.] 4,274

[7.] 71   [8.] 53   [9.] 3,274

                           [10.] 98

Page 198: <u>Final Exam in Long Division with</u>
<u>Modern Methods</u>

[1.] 389   [2.] 49   [3.] 34

[4.] 341   [5.] 897   [6.] 479

          [7.] 94   [8.] 2,003

[9.] 149 (remainder: 346)   [10.] 4,809 (remainder: 1)

CHAPTER 9

INSTANT PROOF!

Page 203: <u>Drill No. 1 on Figuring Digital Roots</u>

[1.] 5   [2.] 5   [3.] 5   [4.] 5

[5.] 5   [6.] 5   [7.] 5   [8.] 6

[9.] 6   [10.] 6   [11.] 1   [12.] 4

[13.] 1   [14.] 1   [15.] 5   [16.] 7

[17.] 4   [18.] 8   [19.] 5   [20.] 5

Page 210: <u>Drill No. 1 in Checking with Digital Roots</u>

| 1. | 2,105 (d.r. — 8) | | 2. | 1,714 (d.r. — 4) |

1. 2,105 (d.r. — 8)   2. 1,714 (d.r. — 4)

3. 1,965 (d.r. — 3)   4. 4,139 (d.r. — 8 + 1 = 9)

5. 3,432 (d.r. — 3 + 4 = 7)

6. 2,237 (d.r. — 5 + 9 = 5)

7. 2,072 (d.r. — 2)   8. 4,582 (d.r. — 1)

9. 8,245 (d.r. — 1)   10. 13 (d.r. — 4 × 8 = 5)

11. $39\frac{16}{47}$ (d.r. — 3 × 2 + 7 = 4)

12. $108\frac{15}{39}$ (d.r. — 9 × 3 + 6 = 6)

Page 214: <u>Drill No. 2 in Figuring Digital Roots — Faster</u>

1. 1	2. 2	3. 2	4. 2	5. 9
6. 6	7. 7	8. 4	9. 4	10. 7
11. 5	12. 9	13. 3	14. 9	15. 9
16. 9	17. 1	18. 2	19. 3	20. 4

Page 220: <u>Final Drill in Figuring Digital Roots — the Fastest Way</u>

1. 6	2. 8	3. 2	4. 4	5. 5
6. 3	7. 5	8. 7	9. 7	10. 6
11. 6	12. 2	13. 9	14. 8	15. 4
16. 8	17. 9	18. 2	19. 4	20. 9

Pages 222 - 228: <u>Final Exam in All Procedures</u>
<u>of Modern Mathematics</u>

1.	557	2.	30,890	3.	1,392
4.	693	5.	3,151	6.	3,003
7.	22,235	8.	16	9.	851
10.	414	11.	254,772	12.	6,438
13.	299,886	14.	3,080	15.	3,072
16.	25,456	17.	7	18.	89
19.	3,626	20.	29,564	21.	505
22.	49	23.	8,430	24.	389,909
25.	8,716	26.	8	27.	3,695
28.	430	29.	67,442	30.	925,756
31.	15,466	32.	33	33.	69
34.	18,012	35.	44,104	36.	723

37. 47 (remainder: 4) 38. 3,108

39. 348,887 40. 278,334

41. 87 (remainder: 11) 42. 43 (remainder: 2)

43. 42,186 44. 51,613

45. 18,283 46. 76,291

47. 349 (remainder: 23) 48. 11 (remainder: 4)

49. 87 (remainder: 17) 50. 364 (remainder: 4)